NEW Close-up
English in Use

B2

David McKeegan

Additional material: Helen Kidd

NATIONAL GEOGRAPHIC LEARNING

Australia • Brazil • Canada • Mexico • Singapore • United Kingdom • United States

Contents

Unit	Grammar	Vocabulary and Use of English
13 pages 90–95	the passive	phrasal verbs; prepositions; collocations and expressions; words easily confused; word formation; sentence transformation
14 pages 96–100	causatives	phrasal verbs; prepositions; collocations and expressions; words easily confused; word formation; sentence transformation
15 pages 101–106	conditionals	phrasal verbs; prepositions; collocations and expressions; words easily confused; word formation; sentence transformation
16 pages 107–111	mixed conditionals; conditionals without *if*	phrasal verbs; prepositions; collocations and expressions; words easily confused; word formation; sentence transformation
Review 4 pages 112–116	B2 Practice: First (Parts 1–4) B2 Practice: ECCE (Grammar and Vocabulary)	
17 pages 117–121	relative clauses	phrasal verbs; prepositions; collocations and expressions; words easily confused; word formation; sentence transformation
18 pages 122–126	reduced relative clauses; participle clauses	phrasal verbs; prepositions; collocations and expressions; words easily confused; word formation; sentence transformation
19 pages 127–133	reported speech	phrasal verbs; prepositions; collocations and expressions; words easily confused; word formation; sentence transformation
20 pages 134–138	reporting verbs	phrasal verbs; prepositions; collocations and expressions; words easily confused; word formation; sentence transformation
Review 5 pages 139–143	B2 Practice: First (Parts 1–4) B2 Practice: ECCE (Grammar and Vocabulary)	
21 pages 144–149	comparative and superlative structures; *so, such, too, enough*	phrasal verbs; prepositions; collocations and expressions; words easily confused; word formation; sentence transformation
22 pages 150–155	gradable and ungradable adjectives; adjectives and adverbs	phrasal verbs; prepositions; collocations and expressions; words easily confused; word formation; sentence transformation
23 pages 156–161	wishes; other ways of talking about unreal situations	phrasal verbs; prepositions; collocations and expressions; words easily confused; word formation; sentence transformation
24 pages 162–166	negative inversion	phrasal verbs; prepositions; collocations and expressions; words easily confused; word formation; sentence transformation
Review 6 pages 167–171	B2 Practice: First (Parts 1–4) B2 Practice: ECCE (Grammar and Vocabulary)	

Awareness

1 Which of these sentences are correct (C) and incorrect (I)?

1 Are you knowing my friend Sam? ____
2 Sally loves reading bestsellers. ____
3 I'm thinking about going to university. ____
4 You're seeming unhappy. What's wrong? ____
5 We live in the countryside. ____
6 I'm not understanding this documentary. ____
7 What do you think about at the moment? ____
8 The train leaves at 9.20. ____
9 The teacher is always shouting at us. ____
10 Oh dear! It rains very heavily now. ____

How many did you get right? ▢

Grammar

Present simple

Affirmative	Negative	Questions
I / We / You / They **work.** He / She / It **works.**	I / We / You / They **don't** work. He / She / It **doesn't** work.	**Do** I / we / you / they **work?** **Does** he / she / it **work?**
Short answers		
Yes, I / we / you / they **do.** **Yes,** he / she / it **does.**	**No,** I / we / you / they **don't.** **No,** he / she / it **doesn't.**	

We use the present simple for:

- facts or general truths.
*The sun **sets** in the west.*

- routines or habits (often with adverbs of frequency).
*Charlotte **rides** her bike to school every day.*

- permanent states.
*Her family **lives** in Germany.*

- timetabled events in the future.
*The train to London **leaves** at 10.30 on Sunday.*

- narratives (a story, a joke, a plot, sports commentaries, etc.).
*Two men **walk** into a restaurant ...*

Note

Some common time expressions that are often used with the present simple are: *every day / week / month / summer, every other day, once a week, twice a month, at the weekend, in January, in the morning / afternoon / evening, at night, on Tuesdays, on Friday mornings, etc.*
*John **goes** to the gym **twice a week.***

Remember

We often use adverbs of frequency with the present simple. They tell us how often something happens. They come before the main verb, but after the verb *be*.
*My basketball team **rarely loses.***
*Janet **is often** late for her music lessons.*

Some common adverbs of frequency are: *always, usually, often, sometimes, rarely / hardly ever / seldom, never.*

Present continuous

Affirmative	Negative	Questions
I **am ('m) work**ing. He / She / It **is ('s) work**ing. We / You / They **are ('re) work**ing.	I **am ('m) not work**ing. He / She / It **is not (isn't) work**ing. We / You / They **are not (aren't) work**ing.	**Am** I **work**ing? **Is** he / she / it **work**ing? **Are** we / you / they **work**ing?
Short answers		
Yes, I **am.** Yes, he / she / it **is.** Yes, we / you / they **are.**	No, I'm **not.** No, he / she / it **isn't.** No, we / you / they **aren't.**	

Spelling: ride → rid**ing**, travel → trave**lling**, study → study**ing**

We use the present continuous for:

- actions that are in progress at the time of speaking.
Irene is playing football at the moment.

- actions that are in progress around the time of speaking, but not right now.
I'm looking for a new house.

- situations that are temporary.
The kids are staying with their uncle until Saturday.

- an annoying habit (often with *always, continually, constantly* and *forever*).
Our maths teacher is always forgetting to mark our homework.

- what is happening in a picture.
Two boys are climbing a tree.

- plans and arrangements for the future.
I'm going to the bank this afternoon.

- situations that are changing or developing in the present.
Computers are getting faster and faster.

> **Note**
>
> Some common time expressions that are often used with the present continuous are: *at the moment, now, for the time being, this morning / afternoon / evening / week / month / year, today,* etc.
> *Tonya is having a bath **at the moment**.*

Stative verbs

Some verbs are not usually used in continuous tenses. They are called *stative verbs* because they describe states and not actions. The most common are:

- verbs of emotion: *hate, like, love, need, prefer, want.*
*I **don't like** greedy people.*

- verbs of senses: *feel, hear, see, smell, sound, taste.*
*You **sound** upset, Kevin.*

- verbs which express a state of mind: *believe, doubt, forget, imagine, know, remember, seem, suppose, think, understand.*
*I **don't understand** Spanish.*

- verbs of possession: *belong to, have, own, possess.*
*Simon **owns** three laptops.*

- other verbs: *be, consist, contain, cost, include, mean.*
*Does the price of the room **include** breakfast?*

Some verbs can be both stative verbs and action verbs, but with a different meaning. The most common are:

be	Michael **is** very kind to his baby sister. (usual behaviour) The children **are being** very well-behaved. (at the moment; not their normal behaviour)
expect	I **expect** you want to eat now. (expect = think or believe) We're **expecting** a delivery this morning. (expect = wait for)
have	Imogen **has** a lot of clothes. (have = own / possess) I'm **having** trouble with my maths homework. (have = experience)
look	You **look** happy. What happened? (look = seem) I'm **looking** for my glasses. (look = search)
taste	This coffee **tastes** strange! (taste = have a particular flavour) I'm **tasting** the sauce in case it needs more sugar. (taste = test the flavour)
think	Do you **think** this is a good film? (think = have an opinion) Mary **is thinking** of changing jobs. (think = consider)
see	I'm sorry, but I **don't see** the point of this. (see = understand) We're **seeing** Charlie on Thursday. (see = meet)
smell	Mmm! Dinner **smells** great! (smell = have a particular smell) I'm **smelling** the meat because I think it is old. (smell = action of smelling)
weigh	I **weigh** 90 kilos. (weigh = have a particular weight) I'm **weighing** myself in the bathroom. (weigh = measure the weight)

1

Grammar exercises

2 Choose the correct option to complete the sentences.

1 He *tastes* / *is tasting* the soup at the moment to see if it needs more salt.
2 They *are visiting* / *visit* their grandparents every Sunday.
3 What *do you think* / *are you thinking* the best way to overcome stress is?
4 Please be quiet. I *am trying* / *try* to concentrate.
5 I can't come with you to the exhibition because I *am seeing* / *see* an old friend.
6 He *is thinking* / *thinks* of buying a house in the country.
7 This perfume *smells* / *is smelling* awful.
8 Jack always *is wearing* / *wears* a helmet when he rides.
9 That isn't true. I *am not believing* / *don't believe* it.
10 Martha *stays* / *is staying* with Julia for the time being.

3 Complete the sentences with the present simple or present continuous form of the verbs.

1 Mrs Owen _____ (receive) a letter from her son every month. He _____ (study) abroad and _____ (never / forget) to write to her.
2 When people _____ (talk) loudly on the phone, I _____ (feel) annoyed.
3 Sam _____ (find) it difficult to remember new words after studying them. He _____ (not / seem) to be able to learn them.
4 She _____ (watch) TV at the moment. She _____ (watch) TV every night to relax before she _____ (go) to bed.
5 Kate can't come to the phone because she _____ (wash) her hair. She _____ (wash) her hair every day.
6 _____ (you / always / lock) your windows before you leave?
7 Look! It _____ (snow). It _____ (rarely / snow) at this time of year.
8 Dan _____ (see) a doctor about his headaches tomorrow morning.

4 Complete the questions with the present simple or present continuous.

1 **A:** Where _____ ?
   B: I usually go to the recording studio at the weekend.
2 **A:** What time _____ ?
   B: I go to the gym at five o'clock every day.
3 **A:** Where _____ ?
   B: My sister works in London.
4 **A:** What _____ on Saturday night?
   B: I'm attending a lecture on climate change.
5 **A:** _____ with us to the party on Sunday?
   B: No, I'm not. I think I will stay at home.
6 **A:** Why _____ that woolly hat?
   B: It was a present from my aunt, and I'm meeting her in five minutes.
7 **A:** _____ a heavy coat?
   B: No, I don't. I only wear a heavy coat when it is cold outside.
8 **A:** What _____ right now?
   B: I'm rewriting my history essay.

5 Rewrite the sentences using the question form. Then complete the short answers.

1 My parents eat out during the week.
A: _____ ?
B: No, _____ .

2 We are going to a concert today.
A: _____ ?
B: No, _____ .

3 Sue is sitting her exams in June.
A: _____ ?
B: Yes, _____ .

4 It snows in the Sahara Desert.
A: _____ ?
B: No, _____ .

5 Paul likes chocolate pancakes.
A: _____ ?
B: Yes, _____ .

6 She comes home from work at 7 p.m.
A: _____ ?
B: No, _____ .

6 Correct the sentences where necessary. Tick those which do not need correcting.

1 Does Emily cycles to work every day?
_____

2 My father always telling us not to eat junk food.
_____

3 What time do the last train leave?
_____

4 She is seeing the dentist at 4 p.m. today.
_____

5 Nobody thinks that John will pass the exam.
_____

6 My brother don't have a job right now.
_____

7 My friend isn't liking her new running shoes.
_____

8 Maria thinks of doing a bungee jump.
_____

7 Complete the sentences with one word in each gap.

1 Why _____ you always borrowing my laptop?
2 We _____ going to the baseball game next week.
3 Kick off for the match _____ at 12.30.
4 My little brother _____ getting taller every month.
5 I'm _____ leaving until this problem is solved.
6 _____ that boy laughing or crying?
7 _____ you appreciate how hard I have been working?
8 That _____ not surprise me at all!

1

Vocabulary

Phrasal verbs

8 Match the phrasal verbs (1–8) with their meanings (a–h).

1 cheer up / cheer (somebody) up ☐   **a** make someone sad
2 chill out ☐   **b** stop liking
3 fall out ☐   **c** relax
4 get (somebody) down ☐   **d** be friendly with someone
5 go off (something / somebody) ☐   **e** not meet someone you've arranged to meet
6 hit it off ☐   **f** feel happier, or make someone feel happier
7 put up with ☐   **g** have an argument and stop being friends
8 stand (somebody) up ☐   **h** tolerate

9 Complete the sentences with the correct form of the phrasal verbs from Exercise 8.

1 I used to like them, but I _____ them after their last song.
2 I've had a hard day at work, so I just want to _____ in front of the TV this evening.
3 Jake waited half an hour for Emma, but she _____ him _____ . He was angry and upset.
4 Mark and Sue _____ last month, and now they aren't speaking to each other.
5 The new teacher will not _____ bad behaviour in her class.
6 Sonja looks very sad. Let's try to _____ her _____ .
7 Simon and Ben _____ it _____ the first time they met because they like the same music.
8 This wet weather is _____ me _____ . I want to go to the beach!

Phrasal verbs

10 Choose the correct option to complete the sentences.

1 Failing the test is nothing to be ashamed *of / with*.
2 This kind of music really gets *on / up* my nerves.
3 Deep *under / down*, she knew that she had made a mistake.
4 She used to be a keen hockey player, but last year she broke her leg *at / in* two places.
5 I was *with / under* the impression that you didn't approve of violent films.
6 My cousin Sarah has to be *at / to* the airport at five o'clock.

Collocations and expressions

11 Choose the correct option to complete the sentences.

1 Greg's mother thinks his friends are a *wrong / bad* influence on him.
2 John's first girlfriend *broke / cracked* his heart when she left him.
3 I can't *face / head* doing any more work today. I'm going home.
4 He was afraid to go on stage because he didn't want to *make / show* a fool of himself.
5 You should know *more / better* than to try and cheat in an exam!
6 Please *convey / express* my apologies to your mum.

Words easily confused

12 Complete the sentences with the correct form of these words. Use each word at least once.

1 **say   speak   talk   tell**

   a   He _____ he was going out, but he didn't _____ me where.

   b   Actions _____ louder than words.

   c   You're _____ nonsense again. Stop _____ lies and start _____ the truth.

   d   What language were they _____ ? I can't _____ the difference between German and Dutch.

   e   Sue _____ us some marvellous stories during her stay.

2 **journey   travel   trip   voyage**

   a   He's away on a business _____ at the moment.

   b   Going on a long sea _____ was dangerous at one time.

   c   The _____ will be shorter once they've completed the tunnel.

   d   _____ is said to broaden the mind.

3 **cost   price   value   worth**

   a   The _____ of living has risen again.

   b   It's _____ far more than I paid for it.

   c   We can't afford a new washing machine at that _____ .

   d   These rare stamps are of great _____ .

4 **blame   error   fault   mistake   wrong**

   a   They sent me two copies of the book in _____ .

   b   It is often quite difficult to tell the difference between right and _____ .

   c   According to her mother, she could do no _____ .

   d   Try not to make so many _____ .

   e   You can't put the _____ on me this time.

   f   I invited her by _____ .

   g   Employing him was a(n) _____ of judgement.

   h   It's not my _____ you lost your wallet.

Word formation   noun → adjective

13 Use the word in capitals to form a word that fits in the gap.

1   I was _____ when I won the competition. I couldn't believe it!   **AMAZEMENT**

2   Tom felt _____ about breaking his brother's headphones.   **GUILT**

3   The players were _____ when they won the match.   **JOY**

4   My brother is quite _____ . He gets upset easily, but he knows when other people are upset, too.   **SENSE**

5   Laura is a very _____ speaker. She enjoys giving presentations.   **CONFIDENCE**

6   Matt is a _____ friend. He always listens to my problems.   **SYMPATHY**

7   Emily is working hard at the moment. She's _____ for a holiday.   **DESPAIR**

8   We were so _____ that no one was hurt in the accident.   **RELIEF**

9   I felt so _____ when everyone was looking at me.   **EMBARRASSMENT**

10   My little sister gets very _____ when she doesn't get what she wants.   **FRUSTRATION**

Sentence transformation

14 Complete the second sentence so that it has a similar meaning to the first sentence, using the word given. Do not change the word given. You must use between two and five words.

1 My brother has the annoying habit of borrowing my socks.

FOREVER

My brother _____ my socks.

2 We used to like this café, but then it changed owners.

WENT

We _____ when it changed owners.

3 The temperature is rising every day.

GETTING

It _____ every day.

4 Sam doesn't want to go out tonight. He's too tired.

FACE

Sam _____ tonight. He's too tired.

5 I thought you enjoyed going for long walks.

UNDER

I _____ that you enjoyed going for long walks.

6 The departure time for the Manchester train is 12.45.

AT

The Manchester train _____ 12.45.

7 It's not your friend's fault that you forgot your homework.

BLAME

You can't put _____ for forgetting your homework.

8 I'm not going to tolerate this ridiculous behaviour any longer.

PUT

I'm not going to _____ this ridiculous behaviour any longer.

Unit 2

1 Which of these sentences are correct (C) and incorrect (I)?

1 He's tired because he's work all day.   ___
2 I haven't saw that play yet.   ___
3 Where have you been all afternoon?   ___
4 Have you ever been bursting into tears in class?   ___
5 Stan has competed in a lot of bicycle races.   ___

6 This is the first time I haven't been passing a maths test!   ___
7 We've been trying to contact you all morning.   ___
8 The prisoner has escaped!   ___
9 Sara hasn't been eating octopus ever before.   ___
10 Your eyes are red. Have you cried?   ___

How many did you get right? ☐

Grammar

Present perfect simple

Affirmative	Negative	Questions
I / We / You / They **have ('ve) eaten**. He / She / It **has ('s) eaten**.	I / We / You / They **have not (haven't) eaten**. He / She / It **has not (hasn't) eaten**.	**Have** I / we / you / they **eaten?** **Has** he / she / it **eaten?**
Short answers		
Yes, I / we / you / they **have**. **Yes**, he / she / it **has**.	**No**, I / we / you / they **haven't**. **No**, he / she / it **hasn't**.	

Spelling: walk → walk**ed**, love → lov**ed**, travel → trave**lled**, ti**dy** → ti**died**, play → play**ed**

We use the present perfect simple:

- for something that started in the past and is still true now.
*We **have worked** here for ten years.*

- for something that happened in the past, but it's not important exactly when.
*Sara **has seen** all of the Marvel films*

- for something that happened in the past and has a direct result that affects the present.
*I'm very hungry because I **haven't eaten** for hours.*

- for an action that finished very recently.
*They **have just done** the dishes.*

- for experiences and achievements.
*He **has run** ten marathons.*

- for an action that has happened several times up to now.
*We**'ve asked** this question many times before.*

- with superlatives.
*It was the best book I **have** ever **read**.*

> **Note**
>
> Some verbs are irregular and do not follow these spelling rules. See a list of irregular verbs and their past participles on pages 172–173.

> **Note**
>
> Some common time expressions that are often used with the present perfect simple are: *already, before, ever, for (ages), just, lately / recently, never, still, yet*, etc.
> *Have you **ever** been to London?*

> **Remember**
>
> We use *have been* when someone has gone somewhere and has now returned. However, we use *have gone* when someone has gone somewhere and is still there.
> *My basketball team **rarely loses**.*
> *Jane **has been** to the gym and now she's at work.*
> *Jane **has gone** to the gym, so try calling her later.*

2

Present perfect continuous

Affirmative	Negative	Questions
I / We / You / They **have ('ve) been** playing. He / She / It **has ('s) been** playing.	I / We / You / They **have not (haven't) been** playing. He / She / It **has not (hasn't) been** playing.	**Have** I / we / you / they **been** playing? **Has** he / she / it **been** playing?
Short answers		
Yes, I / we / you / they **have**. **Yes**, he / she / it **has**.	**No**, I / we / you / they **haven't**. **No**, he / she / it **hasn't**.	

Spelling: make → ma**king**, run → ru**nning**, study → stu**dying**

We use the present perfect continuous:

- for actions that started in the past and are still in progress now or have happened repeatedly until now.
*Henry **has been living** in Spain for a long time.*
- for actions that happened repeatedly in the past and have finished recently, but that have results affecting the present.
*Jane has got fitter because she**'s been exercising** every day.*
- to state how long actions have been in progress.
*I**'ve been studying** Spanish literature for two years.*
- for a recent unfinished action.
*I**'ve been thinking** about you.*

> **Note**
>
> Some common time expressions that are often used with the present perfect continuous are: *all day / morning / night / week, for years / a long time / ages, just, lately / recently*.
> *We've been painting the garage **all day**.*

Present perfect simple or continuous

We use the present perfect simple to talk about something we have done or achieved, or an action that is complete. It is also used to say how many times something happened.
*Oliver **has lived** in three different countries.*

We use the present perfect continuous to talk about how long something has been happening. It is not important whether it has finished or not.
*Amy**'s been working** on her project all summer.*

Grammar exercises

2 **Choose the correct option to complete the sentences.**

1 I *haven't been / haven't been going* to a party yet this year.
2 It *has rained / has been raining* all day. It seems it will never stop!
3 People *have called / have been calling* all morning to say 'Happy Birthday' and they are still calling.
4 I *have tried / have been trying* to contact Peter, but his phone is always engaged.
5 She *has done / has been doing* a parachute jump before, but she doesn't think she can do it now.
6 They *have worked / have been working* in the garden all afternoon.
7 The doctor warned James about his poor health, so he *has stopped / has been stopping* eating unhealthy food.
8 We *have missed / have been missing* the bus, so we're walking to school.

3 **Complete the sentences with the present perfect simple or present perfect continuous form of the verbs.**

1 What's all this mess? What _____ (you / do) all morning?

2 _____ (you / finish) cooking your omelette yet?

3 How long _____ (they / study) Spanish?

4 Sorry I'm late. _____ (you / wait) long?

5 Ask John if _____ (he / lock) the garage.

6 I _____ (read) this book before.

7 _____ (Katy / decide) to apply for the job?

8 Who _____ (use) my laptop? They forgot to switch it off again!

4 **Complete the questions.**

1 **A:** How long _____ ?

B: He's been standing outside for ten minutes.

2 **A:** What _____ ?

B: I haven't done anything.

3 **A:** How long _____ ?

B: I've known Elena for four years.

4 **A:** What _____ all afternoon?

B: The boys have been playing basketball all afternoon.

5 **A:** Where _____ ?

B: I haven't hidden your glasses anywhere!

6 **A:** Why _____ ?

B: I've been crying because I've just seen a very sad film.

7 **A:** _____ my toothbrush?

B: No, I haven't. I've got my own toothbrush!

8 **A:** How long _____ ?

B: I've been waiting about half an hour.

5 **Correct the sentences where necessary. Tick those which do not need correcting.**

1 Someone has been cooking in here. I can smell onions.

_____

2 The house has belonged to the family from 40 years.

_____

3 She just has left her office.

_____

4 I've already been writing five emails this morning.

_____

5 It's the first time she is playing tennis with us.

_____

6 We've been tidying the cupboard, but we haven't finished yet.

_____

7 Dan has been missing the bus, so he'll be late.

_____

8 Her eyes are red because she has cried.

_____

6 Complete the sentences with one word in each gap.

1 Our teacher has _____ marking tests all morning.

2 Have you bought your ticket _____ ?

3 Amelia and Mark have been living together _____ nearly three years.

4 This is the first time I have _____ eaten sushi.

5 I need to work tonight because I _____ haven't finished my essay.

6 _____ long have you been trying to access the internet?

7 Has he broken his new toy _____ ? That was quick!

8 Who _____ been stealing my cheese from the fridge?

Vocabulary

Phrasal verbs

7 Match the phrasal verbs (1–8) with their meanings (a–h).

1 bottle up	☐	**a**	suddenly become very afraid or upset
2 burn out	☐	**b**	hide strong emotions
3 calm down	☐	**c**	recover from an illness or an upsetting situation
4 chicken out	☐	**d**	quickly become attracted to somebody
5 fall for	☐	**e**	become less excited
6 finish with	☐	**f**	end a relationship
7 freak out	☐	**g**	become too afraid to do something
8 get over	☐	**h**	become too ill or tired to do any more work

8 Complete the sentences with the correct form of the phrasal verbs from Exercise 7.

1 She _____ him as soon as she met him, and they got married six months later.

2 Steve _____ his girlfriend last month because they kept arguing about money.

3 I was going to jump off the top diving board, but I _____ in the end – it was too high!

4 It is hard to know how Jen is feeling because she always _____ her emotions.

5 I didn't think Harry would mind me borrowing his bike, but he totally _____ because he thought it had been stolen.

6 _____ ! You shouldn't get so excited about things.

7 You need to take a holiday before you completely _____ .

8 It took her a long time to _____ her illness.

Prepositions

9 Complete the sentences with these words. Use each word at least once.

> for   into   on   to

1 I'm not responsible _____ the behaviour of your children!

2 Dan wasn't sure how to respond _____ his friend's suggestion.

3 You need to stop playing games and focus _____ your exam preparation.

4 Emily was so happy when she heard the news that she burst _____ tears.

5 It's hard to concentrate _____ this reading task while the television is on.

6 Travelling together led _____ Ben and Max's friendship becoming stronger.

Collocations and expressions

10 Choose the correct option to complete the sentences.

1 Emily was in *hurt / agony* when she injured her arm in a skiing accident.
2 The film was so exciting – we were on the *edge / corner* of our seats!
3 It really gets under my *skin / hair* when my sister plays loud music.
4 When Zak received his excellent exam results, he was *missed / lost* for words.
5 I'm sad to say that, with *regret / relief*, we can't come to your wedding because we will be on holiday.
6 His parents are divorced, but they are still on good *terms / friends* with each other.

Words easily confused

11 Complete the sentences with the correct form of these words. Use each word at least once.

1 **advise   insist   persuade   suggest**

   a Do you think you can _____ her to lend you her car?
   b He always _____ on staying at the most expensive hotels.
   c Her personal trainer _____ her to do more exercise.
   d Lauren _____ to us that we should leave on Friday night.

2 **client   customer   guest   patient**

   a The hotel _____ panicked when they heard the alarm go off.
   b There were only a few _____ waiting to see the doctor.
   c He's a well-known lawyer whose _____ include showbiz personalities.
   d In order to attract _____ , the shop owner reduced his prices.

3 **pass   spare   spend   waste**

   a How do you _____ your free time?
   b Don't _____ time! You've got a lot of work to do.
   c Can you _____ ten minutes to discuss the camping trip?
   d Time _____ quickly during the holidays.

4 **course   court   pitch   track**

   a It's one of the best golf _____ I've played on.
   b I'm afraid all the tennis _____ are booked.
   c The spectator who ran onto the _____ was removed from the football stadium by police.
   d Athletes enjoy running on _____ where the spectators are close to the action.

5 **burgle   cheat   rob   steal**

   a Her flat has been _____ twice this year.
   b Nobody knows who _____ the laptop.
   c My business partner tried to _____ me out of my share of the profits.
   d Banks in the USA are _____ quite frequently.

2

Word formation adjective → noun

12 Use the word in capitals to form a word that fits in the gap.

1 Our primary concern is for the _____ of the children at this school.   **SAFE**

2 Don't lie to me. I want to hear the _____ .   **TRUE**

3 It's _____ to go swimming in this weather. You'll freeze!   **MAD**

4 Do you know the _____ between an adverb and an adjective?   **DIFFERENT**

5 Most students suffer from _____ before an important exam.   **ANXIOUS**

6 The _____ of mobile apps is increasing all the time.   **POPULAR**

7 It takes a lot of _____ to lift your own weight.   **STRONG**

8 What's the _____ between London and Manchester?   **DISTANT**

9 There was a lot of _____ in the room before the meeting started.   **TENSE**

10 You will need to improve your _____ if you want to compete at this level.   **FIT**

Sentence transformation

13 Complete the second sentence so that it has a similar meaning to the first sentence, using the word given. Do not change the word given. You must use between two and five words.

1 The children aren't here – they're in the park with their uncle.

HAVE

The children _____ with their uncle.

2 They started studying two hours ago, and they're still studying now.

STUDYING

They _____ two hours.

3 I didn't know what to say about Maria's bad news.

LOST

I was _____ about Maria's bad news.

4 The small child suddenly started to cry when he dropped his ice cream.

BURST

The small child _____ when he dropped his ice cream.

5 I'm glad that you two are friendly with each other.

TERMS

I'm glad that you two _____ with each other.

6 He was going to enter the race, but he got scared.

CHICKENED

He _____ entering the race.

7 She ended their relationship on his birthday.

FINISHED

She _____ him on his birthday.

8 After we gave him some food, the baby became quieter.

CALMED

The baby _____ after we gave him some food.

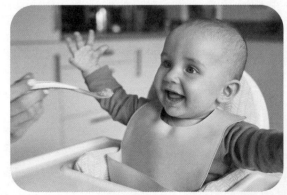

Awareness

1 **Which of these sentences are correct (C) and incorrect (I)?**

1 We cancelled the party because Sami was ill. ___
2 You didn't went home early, did you? ___
3 Everyone agreed it was a great plan. ___
4 What did you doing at eight o'clock last night? ___
5 I would enjoy this cartoon when I was a child. ___

6 My dad teached me how to make pancakes. ___
7 I was working when I heard the celebration. ___
8 Dan used to drive everywhere, but now he cycles. ___
9 Did you used to fight with your brother? ___
10 We were swimming in the lake last Sunday. ___

How many did you get right? ☐

Grammar

Past simple

Affirmative	Negative	Questions
I / He / She / It / We / You / They walk**ed**.	I / He / She / It / We / You / They **didn't** walk.	**Did** I / he / she / it / we / you / they **walk**?
Short answers		
Yes, I / he / she / it / we / you / they **did**.	**No**, I / he / she / it / we / you / they **didn't**.	

Spelling: race → raced, control → contro**lled**, stu**dy** → stu**died**, play → pla**yed**

We use the past simple for:
- something that started and finished in the past.
*Archeologists **discovered** Tutankhamun in 1922.*
- past routines and habits (often with adverbs of frequency).
*We **often visited** the museum when we were children.*
- past states.
*We **loved** living in a different country.*
- actions that happened one after the other in the past, for example when telling a story.
*He **stood up**, **walked** to the window, and **shouted** into the night*

> **Note**
> Some verbs are irregular and do not follow these spelling rules. See a list of irregular verbs on pages 172–173.

> **Note**
> Some common time expressions that are often used with the past simple are: *yesterday, last night / week / month / summer, a week / month / year ago, twice a week, once a month, at the weekend, in March, in the morning / afternoon / evening, at night, on Thursdays, on Monday mornings,* etc.
> *I listened to some great new bands **at the weekend**.*

Past continuous

Affirmative	Negative	Questions
I / He / She / It **was** walk**ing**. We / You / They **were** walk**ing**.	I / He / She / It **was not (wasn't)** walk**ing**. We / You / They **were not (weren't)** walk**ing**.	**Was** I / he / she / it walk**ing**? **Were** we / you / they walk**ing**?
Short answers		
Yes, I / he / she / it **was**. **Yes**, we / you / they **were**.	**No**, I / he / she / it **wasn't**. **No**, we / you / they **weren't**.	

Spelling: shine → shin**ing**, control → contro**lling**, ti**dy** → ti**dying**

3

We use the past continuous for:
- actions that were in progress at a specific time in the past.

*Susan **was walking** home at six o'clock this evening.*
- two or more actions that were in progress at the same time in the past.

*Martin **was reading** while Helen **was watching** TV.*
- giving background information in a story.

*It **was raining**, and a strong wind **was blowing**.*
- an action that was in progress in the past that was interrupted by another action.

*Daniel **was checking** the bill when the waiter **returned** to the table.*
- temporary situations in the past.

*We **were living** in the suburbs of Manchester at the time.*

used to and *would*

We use *used to* + infinitive for:
- actions that happened regularly in the past.

*I **used to collect** plastic dinosaurs.*
- states that existed for a long time in the past.

*Emily **used to like** gold jewellery, but now she prefers silver.*

We use *would* + infinitive for actions that happened regularly in the past. We don't use it for past states.
*During the summer holidays, we **would play** cricket every day until sunset.*

> **Note**
>
> Some common time expressions that are often used with the past continuous are: *while, as, all day / week / month / year, at ten o'clock last night, last Sunday / week / year, this morning*, etc.
> *They were learning about the Romans **this morning**.*

Grammar exercises

2 **Complete the text with the past simple or past continuous form of the verbs.**

I ¹ was _____ (walk) along Regent Street when I ² _____ (realise) that a man ³ _____ (follow) me. I ⁴ _____ (turn) right and he ⁵ _____ (follow). Whenever I ⁶ _____ (stop), he ⁷ _____ (do) too. I ⁸ _____ (decide) to take the 717 bus. Just as it ⁹ _____ (move) off, I ¹⁰ _____ (jump) on. The man ¹¹ _____ (miss) the bus, but he ¹² _____ (get) on another 717. He ¹³ _____ (not / notice) me getting off or heading for the nearest police station.

3 **Use the prompts to write sentences with the past simple, past continuous and *when* or *while*. Start with the words in bold.**

1 **My mother** / watch the news / my father / cook

_____

2 **Kate** / do her homework / I / phone her

_____

3 **Pam** / paint her room / her friend / arrive

_____

4 **I** / read a comic / he / burst into the room

_____

5 **A** lot of people / dance / Max and I / eat snacks

_____

6 **We** / serve the food / it / start raining

_____

4 Complete the exchanges using the words in brackets.

1 **A:** Did he give the present to her? (him)
B: *No, he didn't give the present to her. He gave the present to him.*

2 **A:** Did your mother know about it? (father)
B: _____

3 **A:** Was the dog barking at a cat? (the postman)
B: _____

4 **A:** Did she move here three years ago? (four years ago)
B: _____

5 **A:** Were they celebrating a birthday? (wedding)
B: _____

6 **A:** Did Dan cook you Italian food? (Japanese)
B: _____

7 **A:** Was she wearing a bracelet? (necklace)
B: _____

8 **A:** Did the Aztecs come from Argentina? (Mexico)
B: _____

5 Complete the questions.

1 **A:** _____ at nine o'clock last night?
B: No, I wasn't sleeping. I was reading.

2 **A:** What _____ at ten o'clock this morning?
B: I was queuing outside the Anthropology Museum.

3 **A:** How long _____ ?
B: I taught English in Spain for three years.

4 **A:** Where _____ ?
B: They were at the beach.

5 **A:** Why _____ ?
B: I bought a new phone because it has a better camera.

6 **A:** What _____ ?
B: I was buying tickets to a concert when the internet stopped working.

7 **A:** Why _____ ?
B: I didn't come to the festival because I was at a wedding.

8 **A:** _____ when I called you?
B: No, I wasn't cooking. I was watching an interesting documentary.

6 Choose the correct option to complete the sentences.

1 He *used to / would* have long hair.
2 My father would *to take / take* us out for a meal on his birthday.
3 Did you use to *get / getting* a lot of pocket money?
4 They *would / were used to* send us a postcard every summer.
5 I *would / used to* understand German when I was a child.
6 When I was at primary school, I *would / use to* go to bed at eight o'clock.
7 My grandmother *would / used to* have enormous gold earrings.
8 Every year, Mum would *make / to make* birthday cakes in the shape of our age.

3

7 Complete the sentences with one word in each gap.

1 _____ you hear about the new exhibition at the art gallery?

2 The sun _____ shining brightly when we woke up the next morning.

3 I was composing a song _____ Jane was writing a poem.

4 Did you use _____ enjoy dressing up as a pirate when you were younger?

5 I watched a documentary about clothes and culture, and _____ I went to bed.

6 _____ didn't you go to school yesterday?

7 _____ long have you been trying to book tickets online?

8 Where did Tina go _____ night?

Vocabulary

Phrasal verbs

8 Match the phrasal verbs (1–8) with their meanings (a–h).

1 call round ☐   **a** telephone somebody again

2 call (somebody) back ☐   **b** discover by accident

3 call off ☐   **c** remember, think about the past

4 come across ☐   **d** become available to buy

5 come along ☐   **e** visit somebody's house

6 come out ☐   **f** go somewhere with somebody

7 date back ☐   **g** cancel an event

8 look back at ☐   **h** exist since a particular time in the past

9 Complete the sentences with the correct form of the phrasal verbs from Exercise 8.

1 We're going to the festival in the park. Why don't you _____ with us?

2 If I don't answer the first time, _____ me _____ in half an hour.

3 We're very excited that our first song is _____ next week.

4 She was clearing out the attic when she _____ an old photo of her grandparents.

5 The tradition of decorating trees at Christmas _____ to Germany in the 16th century.

6 I'll _____ to your house this evening.

7 You can learn a lot when you _____ your mistakes.

8 The outdoor concert was _____ because of the rain.

Prepositions

10 Choose the correct option to complete the sentences.

1 We cannot lose this competition. We must win *at / by / in* all costs.

2 That was *at / by / in* far the dullest book I have ever read in my life.

3 *At / By / In* general, I think foreign travel makes people respect other cultures more.

4 I am writing to you *at / by / in* connection with my project on tribal costumes.

5 She knows the recipe *at / by / in* heart because she makes it so often.

6 We will have a car *at / by / in* our disposal for the duration of our stay.

Collocations and expressions

11 **Choose the correct option to complete the sentences.**

1 Mr Wilson has *built / given* a reputation as an expert in Native American history

2 Some traditional designs are protected. You can't *use / know* them without permission.

3 The festival of Halloween *has / holds* its roots in Celtic and Roman festivals.

4 The internet *saved / played* an important role in our research for this project.

5 Thankfully, the earthquake didn't *do / have* much damage to the museum.

6 The Romans *did / built* an empire that stretched from the Atlantic to the Middle East.

Words easily confused

12 **Complete the sentences with the correct form of these words. Use each word at least once.**

1 | audience   crowd   gang   listener   member   spectator   viewer |

    a The police had difficulty in controlling the _____ that had turned up to greet the singer at the airport.

    b _____ will be able to take part in the TV discussion programme.

    c Radio 1 _____ should tune in at four o'clock for live coverage of the festival.

    d The _____ thoroughly enjoyed the play.

    e Fewer than 1,000 _____ saw the game.

    f Every _____ of the family brought food for Grandad's party.

    g After the robbery, the _____ escaped in a stolen car.

2 | artificial   fake   false   imitation |

    a Jackets made of _____ leather are much cheaper than those made of genuine leather.

    b There was no fire. It was a(n) _____ alarm.

    c He lost his job when it was discovered that his diploma was a(n) _____ .

    d It wasn't a real Ming vase – it was just a cheap _____ .

3 | achieve   fulfil   manage   succeed |

    a She _____ success very early in her career.

    b We _____ to complete the project in one week.

    c Robert never _____ the promise he showed as a young pianist.

    d William _____ in discovering the truth.

4 | bargain   chance   occasion   opportunity   situation |

    a The offer of a job abroad was a golden _____ for me to make a fresh start.

    b The scarf was a(n) _____ at £10.

    c What are the _____ of you getting a job in the music industry?

    d It was a(n) _____ on which all the family could celebrate.

    e We've got a problem to solve, so let's look at the _____ , shall we?

3

Word formation mixed

13 Use the word in capitals to form a word that fits in the gap.

1 What are the _____ of this celebration? **ORIGINAL**

2 It was a big wedding. There were 200 guests at the _____ . **RECEIVE**

3 The dancing and other _____ continued until very late. **FESTIVE**

4 Almost every culture has _____ based on food and eating. **TRADITIONAL**

5 The fireworks on New Year's Eve were an amazing _____ . **SPECTATE**

6 The festival can be very loud, so it isn't _____ for young children. **SUIT**

7 The shirt is available in _____ patterns and colours. **VARY**

8 Clothes and jewellery are _____ in many different cultures. **SIGNIFY**

Sentence transformation

14 Complete the second sentence so that it has a similar meaning to the first sentence, using the word given. Do not change the word given. You must use between two and five words.

1 I climbed trees when I was a young boy.
   USED
   When I was a young boy, _____ trees.

2 I'll phone you again later, when I have more time.
   CALL
   I'll _____ when I have more time.

3 She cancelled her birthday party when she became ill.
   OFF
   When she became ill, she _____ her birthday party.

4 You must do everything you can to succeed tomorrow.
   COSTS
   You must succeed _____ tomorrow.

5 I've never seen a film that was nearly as exciting as that one.
   FAR
   That _____ the most exciting film I've ever seen.

6 The festival always takes place on the last weekend of July.
   HELD
   The festival _____ on the last weekend of July.

7 I found this by accident when I was cleaning your room.
   ACROSS
   I _____ when I was cleaning your room.

8 This tradition started in the 17th century.
   DATES
   This tradition _____ to the 17th century.

Unit 4

Awareness

1 Which of these sentences are correct (C) and incorrect (I)?

1 Our cat has disappeared last week. ____
2 Oh no! I've lost my mobile phone. ____
3 This band hasn't released a good song since 2018. ____
4 Nobody has ever spoke to me like that. ____
5 We haven't heard from Rob since ages. ____
6 I've known Charlie for seven years. ____
7 How long ago did you take up the piano? ____
8 I been on holiday to Morocco last summer. ____
9 He's use to travelling alone. ____
10 I've been getting used to the new computer system. ____

How many did you get right? ☐

Grammar

Past simple and present perfect

We use the past simple for actions that happened at a specified time in the past and we think of as finished.
*I **read** an article about space travel last night.*
*She **worked** in a museum for two years. (She no longer works there.)*

We use the present perfect for actions that happened at an unspecified time in the past and for actions or situations that began in the past and are still in progress or have an effect on the present.
*Steven **has written** a poem for his girlfriend. (We don't know or don't say when.)*
*The children **have been** at the swimming pool all afternoon. (They are still at the swimming pool.)*

be used to and get used to

We use *be used to* + verb + *-ing* form / noun to talk about actions and states which are usual or familiar.
*Andy **is used to working** at night because he has been doing it for ages.*

We use *get used to* + verb + *-ing* form / noun to talk about actions and states which are becoming more familiar.
*The students **are getting used to the new head teacher's rules**.*

> **Note**
>
> With *used to*, the verbs *be* and *get* change depending on the tense that is needed in the context.
> *I **was used to** hot weather because I had been living in Egypt for many years.*
> *I **have been getting used to** going to bed early.*

Grammar exercises

2 Choose the correct option to complete the sentences.

1 Martin *hasn't finished / didn't finish* writing his novel yet.
2 Mrs Black *has taught / taught* history last year.
3 Anna still *hasn't found / didn't find* her earring.
4 Archeologists *discovered / have discovered* the plates many years ago.
5 *I've been / I've gone* to the art exhibition. Look what I bought!
6 Our neighbours have moved. *They've been / They've gone* to live in Australia.
7 I'm not used to *tell / telling* other people what to do.
8 My brother *gets / is* used to doing his homework in the morning.
9 Have you *got / been* used to living in the city yet?
10 She has great difficulty in *being / getting* used to living alone.

3 Complete the sentences with these words. Use each word at least once.

| ago | already | ever | for | just | recently | still | yet |

1 I haven't finished decorating the house

_____ .

2 I have _____ bought these earrings. Do you like them?

3 I haven't seen John _____ a while.

4 She started playing the violin three years

_____ .

5 She _____ hasn't finished cooking. The guests have already arrived!

6 We'll have to choose another film. I have _____ seen this one.

7 Have you _____ visited an old castle?

8 I have been having terrible headaches

_____ .

4 Correct the sentences where necessary. Tick those which do not need correcting.

1 It is been three years since I last went on holiday.

_____

2 Nobody has ever been here before.

_____

3 How long ago did you came to this city?

_____

4 Laura has lost her passport last week.

_____

5 We haven't heard from Simon for a long time.

_____

6 When have you sent the tickets? I haven't received them yet.

_____

7 I could get use to living in a luxury apartment.

_____

8 They aren't used to eating out every night.

_____

5 Complete the sentences with the past simple or present perfect form of the verbs.

1 Since I _____ (leave) school two years ago, I _____ (not / see) Jenny.

2 I _____ (never / eat) this kind of food before.

3 Sam _____ (not / go) to a concert since he _____ (be) 20.

4 A: _____ (you / ever / fly) a helicopter?

B: Yes, I _____ (fly) a helicopter when I was in the air force.

5 Last week, Jim _____ (finish) one of the best pictures he _____ (ever / paint).

6 Katy _____ (go) to live in the country six months ago and _____ (not / be) back since then.

6 Complete the sentences with the correct form of *be used to* or *get used to*.

1 I find it difficult to _____ driving on the left. I think it will take me some time.

2 Mark will never _____ the cold winters in Canada after living in California.

3 The students _____ studying hard as their teacher is very demanding.

4 I _____ having orange juice and eggs for breakfast.

5 You'll soon _____ speaking Spanish every day when you move to Spain.

6 She _____ (not) working so late into the night.

7 Write questions for the answers.

1 A: _____ ?
   B: I've lived in this town for five years.

2 A: _____ ?
   B: Tom travelled round Europe two years ago.

3 A: _____ ?
   B: We camped in the forest last night.

4 A: _____ ?
   B: Yes, I have written a film review before.

5 A: _____ ?
   B: Yes, the teacher marked our test last night.

6 A: _____ ?
   B: No, he hasn't spoken to her yet.

7 A: _____ ?
   B: Yes, she's used to swimming in cold water.

8 A: _____ ?
   B: No, I'm not getting used to living in a hot climate.

Vocabulary

Phrasal verbs

8 Match the phrasal verbs (1–8) with their meanings (a–h).

1	call for	☐	**a**	ask
2	call on	☐	**b**	start to do something
3	come to	☐	**c**	require or demand
4	come up	☐	**d**	understand, feel the same as
5	go ahead	☐	**e**	be mentioned in a conversation
6	identify with	☐	**f**	persuade somebody to do something
7	spread out over	☐	**g**	total, when added together
8	talk (somebody) into	☐	**h**	happening over a long period of time

9 Complete the sentences with the correct form of the phrasal verbs from Exercise 8.

1 That meal was quite cheap. The bill _____ £35.50.

2 The issue of cultural identity _____ in the discussion about school uniform.

3 Having a shared interest, like music, can help you _____ people from other cultures.

4 The organisers of the festival are planning to _____ , despite the wind and rain.

5 The audience _____ the author of the play to come on stage.

6 Zak's friends _____ him _____ performing in the concert.

7 I can afford the trip because the payments are _____ six months.

8 Walking in the mountains _____ a high level of fitness and warm, waterproof clothing!

4

Prepositions

10 **Choose the correct option to complete the sentences.**

1 He admitted that he was *at / in / by* fault, and apologised to the taxi driver.
2 The weather is getting warmer day *at / in / by* day.
3 I am very much *at / in / by* favour of students spending a year abroad.
4 She said that she found the novel 'unsatisfying' – *at / in / by* other words, she hated it.
5 The cost of air travel has increased *at / in / by* 20% in the past two years.
6 If your house is too close to the river, it is *at / in / by* risk of flooding.

Collocations and expressions

11 **Choose the correct option to complete the sentences.**

1 The carnival in Rio de Janeiro is widely *done / known* as one of the biggest festivals in the world.
2 We spent years *playing / building* a good relationship with our neighbours.
3 The festival is *held / had* every summer in a farmer's fields.
4 You'll *know / save* a lot of space if you give away some of the clothes you don't wear anymore.
5 I'm not sure how I'm going to deal with this situation – I'll just have to *use / play* it by ear.
6 The best man at my brother's wedding *gave / built* a very funny speech!

Words easily confused

12 **Complete the sentences with the correct form of these words. Use each word at least once.**

1 | beat   earn   gain   win |

  a I think we can _____ his team in the final.
  b She _____ some money at the horse races.
  c The director is said to _____ about £10,000 a month.
  d Who _____ the music competition last year?
  e Sally's mother says she's not losing a daughter, but _____ a son.

2 | forget   leave   lose   miss |

  a We'll be late if we _____ the early train.
  b Have you _____ your book at home again?
  c Could I borrow a pencil? I've _____ mine. It's in my other pencil case.
  d I can't find my sunglasses anywhere. I suppose I must have _____ them.

3 | deny   refrain   refuse   reject   resist |

  a I _____ to help people who won't help themselves.
  b Although the cakes looked delicious, I _____ the temptation to eat one.
  c How can he _____ losing the ring when he had it last?
  d All my job applications have been _____ .
  e Would visitors please _____ from touching the paintings?

4 | manner   path   route   way |

  a Do you know the _____ to the cathedral?
  b If we go by the shortest _____ , we'll get there by midday.
  c I enjoy walking along the _____ in Sherwood Forest.
  d She has such a charming _____ .

5 origin   source   stock   supply

  a Nobody knows the _____ of the word.

  b I'll check to see if we have those earrings in _____ .

  c The rain and floods affected the country's food _____ .

  d Explorers couldn't find the _____ of the river.

Word formation   noun → verb

13 Use the word in capitals to form a word that fits in the gap.

  1 All my dad's old CDs are _____ according to musical type.   **CLASS**

  2 Can you _____ that you were at the cinema last night?   **PROOF**

  3 Many medical conditions can be _____ by art or music, as well as medicines.   **RELIEF**

  4 We _____ students to make use of our excellent library.   **COURAGE**

  5 I hope you _____ in your ambition to become a professional dancer.   **SUCCESS**

  6 The newspaper was forced to _____ for printing incorrect information.   **APOLOGY**

  7 Don't let the dog out, or it will _____ the children.   **TERROR**

  8 He doesn't like it if you _____ his work.   **CRITIC**

Sentence transformation

14 Complete the second sentence so that it has a similar meaning to the first sentence, using the word given. Do not change the word given. You must use between two and five words.

  1 She started to live here two years ago.
    FOR
    She _____ two years.

  2 I haven't seen Tonya for three weeks.
    TIME
    The _____ Tonya was three weeks ago.

  3 He approves of children learning to play musical instruments.
    FAVOUR
    He _____ children learning to play musical instruments.

  4 In the meeting, someone suggested having an art exhibition.
    UP
    The suggestion of an art exhibition _____ in the meeting.

  5 There's a danger that you will injure yourself on this climb.
    RISK
    You are _____ yourself on this climb.

  6 The last time we performed was last July.
    SINCE
    We _____ last July.

  7 You were not to blame for the accident.
    FAULT
    You were _____ for the accident.

  8 You need a lot of patience to do this task.
    CALLS
    This task _____ patience.

Part 1

For questions 1–8, read the text below and decide which answer (A, B, C or D) best fits each gap. There is an example at the beginning (0).

Stockholm syndrome

Imagine the following **(0)** ___ . A gang of bank robbers cannot escape because police have surrounded the building. Automatically, the **(1)** ___ become hostages, while the criminals **(2)** ___ time deciding what to do. Outside the bank a crowd has gathered, with TV crews providing **(3)** ___ with live coverage of the incident. Back inside the building, a relationship is developing between the hostages and their captors. They start **(4)** ___ each other about themselves and the hostages begin to put the blame for the incident on the police and authorities.

You may think that this is a scene from a Hollywood movie, but you would be **(5)** ___ . The phenomenon is **(6)** ___ as 'Stockholm Syndrome' because it was first observed in Stockholm, Sweden. The hostages helped their captors solve any problems that **(7)** ___ up, and even protected their captors when they all left the building together. Nobody knows quite what **(8)** ___ this behaviour, but it seems that the value of communication cannot be overestimated.

0	**A** condition	**(B)** situation	**C** happening	**D** state
1	**A** guests	**B** customers	**C** buyers	**D** clients
2	**A** pass	**B** spare	**C** do	**D** spend
3	**A** viewers	**B** spectators	**C** listeners	**D** readers
4	**A** talking	**B** telling	**C** speaking	**D** saying
5	**A** false	**B** wrong	**C** missing	**D** off
6	**A** called	**B** described	**C** known	**D** named
7	**A** came	**B** held	**C** stayed	**D** moved
8	**A** sets	**B** brings	**C** makes	**D** causes

Part 2

For questions 9–16, read the text below and think of the word which best fits each gap. Use only one word in each gap. There is an example at the beginning (0).

Some spare-time activities

Spare-time activities basically fall into two categories: traditional (0) ____and____ modern. Traditional activities include pastimes such (9) _____ collecting and reading, while modern activities involve computer games, the internet and television.

Children often become interested in collecting when they come (10) _____ something their parents or grandparents have collected. Although they might be keen (11) _____ collecting when they first start, they very often become fed up with it when they reach their teens. Reading is a leisure activity that develops with parental encouragement. Unlike collecting, reading is a pastime that people hardly (12) _____ abandon.

Nowadays, it is not unusual to find a teenager's bedroom full (13) _____ electronic devices and computer games. While computer games (14) _____ considered to be mainly a teenage pastime, social media and browsing the internet are popular with both teenagers and adults. Another pastime which teenagers have (15) _____ common with adults is watching television. Interestingly, none of these activities involve having a discussion about important issues – something which was popular in (16) _____ past.

Part 3

For questions 17–24, read the text below. Use the word given in capitals at the end of some of the lines to form a word that fits in the gap in the same line. There is an example at the beginning (0).

Bringing families closer

A recent survey conducted by a leading scientific magazine has (0) ____surprisingly____ revealed **SURPRISE**

that electronic devices do not weaken relationships within families. In fact, the opposite is true –

they actually bring children and parents together.

There has been a huge (17) _____ in the number of parents who have become **GROW**

involved in their children's (18) _____ activities online. This appears to **EDUCATE**

(19) _____ bonds between family members, as they work and play together on a **STRONG**

range of devices.

One further (20) _____ reached in a report based on the survey is that children's **CONCLUDE**

(21) _____ needs are satisfied. This occurs because children consistently beat their **COMPETE**

parents at computer-based games. The survey must come as a great (22) _____ **RELIEVE**

to parents, many of whom were originally (23) _____ about the wisdom of **DOUBT**

having so many devices at home. After all, no parent wants their child to become anti-social and

uncommunicative, which used to be a common fear.

Parents no longer have any reason to be (24) _____ of these tools, which now **SUSPECT**

play an essential role in modern life.

Part 4

For questions 25–30, complete the second sentence so that it has a similar meaning to the first sentence, using the word given. Do not change the word given. You must use between two and five words, including the word given. Here is an example (0).

Example:

0 This is my first fishing trip.
NEVER
I _____ *have never been on* _____ a fishing trip before.

25 I first met Sarah twelve years ago, and I still know her now.
FOR
I _____ twelve years.

26 I don't remember Mary being such a difficult person in the past.
USE
Mary _____ such a difficult person.

27 How did you persuade Dad to lend you his car?
TALK
How did you _____ you his car?

28 The growth of these plants was very slow in my back garden.
GROW
These plants _____ in my back garden.

29 I think what she said at the press conference was true.
TRUTH
I think _____ at the press conference.

30 She talks nonsense all the time and I can't stand it.
NERVES
It really _____ that she talks nonsense all the time.

B2 Practice: ECCE

Grammar

For questions 1–20, choose the word or phrase that best completes the sentence or conversation.

1 Simon isn't in. He has ___ to the theatre.
   A been
   B gone
   C went
   D done

2 My laptop ran out of power an hour ___ .
   A ago
   B since
   C away
   D lately

3 Did we ___ go to the same nursery school?
   A would
   B used to
   C use to
   D using to

4 Those jeans ___ too much money!
   A are costing
   B costs
   C is costing
   D cost

5 My cousin ___ in Australia at the moment.
   A studies
   B is studying
   C study
   D is study

6 ___ your ridiculous story.
   A I don't believe
   B I not believe
   C I'm not believing
   D I don't believing

7 Who's been ___ my cheese?
   A ate
   B eaten
   C eating
   D eat

8 We've ___ got past Level 2 of this game.
   A ever
   B no
   C done
   D never

9 I ___ having lunch when the phone rang.
   A am
   B was
   C will
   D did

10 I hope they ___ arguing again yesterday.
   A wasn't
   B aren't
   C didn't
   D weren't

11 I've been having a lot of bad dreams ___ .
   A since
   B recently
   C ever
   D always

12 I've ___ dinner so I'm not hungry.
   A already eaten
   B just ate
   C still eaten
   D never ate

13 They ___ living in the big city.
   A would
   B used to
   C are getting used to
   D are being used to

14 ___ you always brush your teeth at night?
   A Are
   B What
   C Why
   D Do

15 Where ___ your father work?
   A is
   B does
   C are
   D do

16 We saw some great shows ___ year.
   A last
   B ago
   C next
   D once

17 'Do you want to come out?'
   'I haven't finished writing this essay ___ .'
   A still
   B ever
   C yet
   D just

18 'I'm exhausted.'
   '___ you been working all afternoon?'
   A Are
   B Do
   C Did
   D Have

19 Steve ___ basketball for three years.
   A play
   B has played
   C did play
   D is playing

20 We ___ swimming for ages.
   A didn't be
   B weren't
   C haven't
   D haven't been

Vocabulary

For questions 21–40, choose the word or phrase that most appropriately completes the sentence.

21 I can't ___ eating when I'm this ill.
A face
B mouth
C head
D foot

22 I've got so much work to do! It's really getting me ___ .
A in
B on
C up
D down

23 The audience ___ into applause at the end.
A snapped
B banged
C burst
D popped

24 Calm down! There's no need to ___ out.
A run
B freak
C crash
D flash

25 Many music festivals are ___ in the UK every summer.
A had
B given
C played
D held

26 Why don't you come ___ with us to the park?
A under
B along
C for
D round

27 We don't have a plan, so let's just play it by ___ .
A heart
B ear
C nose
D neck

28 You must get into this university at all ___ .
A costs
B prices
C events
D possibilities

29 Did you fall ___ with your best friend again?
A over
B for
C out
D in

30 We were on the ___ of our seats all through the film.
A edge
B side
C corner
D top

31 In other ___ , I don't want to go out tonight.
A words
B verbs
C ways
D things

32 Don't ___ a fool of yourself!
A show
B do
C mark
D make

33 The celebration has its ___ in an ancient tradition.
A nerves
B skin
C roots
D terms

34 I know this poem by ___ .
A head
B mouth
C stomach
D heart

35 You shouldn't ___ up your feelings.
A box
B carton
C pack
D bottle

36 Emma and Anna are great friends. They hit it ___ the first time they met.
A off
B on
C out
D over

37 It took him years to get ___ the loss of his mother.
A out
B over
C off
D on

38 With ___ , we cannot come to your party.
A regret
B agony
C panic
D curiosity

39 I'm sorry, we had to ___ off the meeting.
A tell
B make
C call
D come

40 Despite the rain, the festival is expected to go ___ .
A along
B away
C around
D ahead

Unit 5

Awareness

1 Which of these sentences are correct (C) and incorrect (I)?

1 We had just arrived when the show began. ___	**6** She decided not to go because she hadn't been enjoying it last time. ___	
2 The manager hadn't being informed. ___	**7** We had wrote to them about this before. ___	
3 They had been played non-stop for hours. ___	**8** The children had been swimming all morning. ___	
4 Had you been searching for a long time? ___	**9** I hadn't heard about the new head teacher. ___	
5 The teacher had been waiting for everyone to calm down. ___	**10** He'd been working for age. ___	

How many did you get right? [ ]

Grammar

Past perfect simple

Affirmative	Negative	Questions
I / He / She / It / We / You / They **had ('d) watched.**	I / He / She / It / We / You / They **had not (hadn't) watched.**	**Had** I / he / she / it / we / you / they **watched?**
Short answers		
Yes, I / he / she / it / we / you / they had.	**No**, I / he / she / it / we / you / they hadn't.	

Spelling: walk → walk**ed**, love → love**d**, travel → trave**lled**, study → stu**died**, play → play**ed**

We use the past perfect simple for an action or situation that finished before another action, situation or time in the past.
*I **had watched** every one of her films before I interviewed her.*

> **Note**
>
> Some verbs are irregular and do not follow these spelling rules. See a list of irregular verbs on pages 172–173.

> **Note**
>
> Some common time expressions that are often used with the past perfect simple are: *before, after, when, already, for, for a long time, for ages, just, never, once, since 2019 / July, yet*, etc.
> *The footballer hadn't played **for a long time** because of his injury.*

Past perfect continuous

Affirmative	Negative	Questions
I / He / She / It / We / You / They **had ('d) been reading.**	I / He / She / It / We / You / They **had not (hadn't) been reading.**	**Had** I / he / she / it / we / you / they **been reading?**
Short answers		
Yes, I / he / she / it / we / you / they **had**.	**No**, I / he / she / it / we / you / they **hadn't**.	

Spelling: make → mak**ing**, run → run**ning**, tidy → ti**dying**

We use the past perfect continuous:
- for actions that started in the past and were still in progress when something happened.
*The audience **had been waiting** half an hour before the band came on stage.*
- for actions that were in progress in the past and had an effect on a later action.
*Steve was exhausted because he **had been training** hard all day.*

> **Note**
>
> Some common time expressions that are often used with the past perfect continuous are: *all day / night / week, for years / a long time / ages, since*. We can use *How long ...?* with the past perfect continuous in questions.
> ***How long** had it been raining before they cancelled the tennis tournament?*

5

Grammar exercises

2 **Choose the correct option to complete the sentences.**

1 When her parents arrived, *she had done / had been doing* her homework for three hours.
2 As soon as she got home, she realised she *had left / had been leaving* her glasses at work.
3 My brother *had tried / had been trying* to repair the TV for two hours before I called him.
4 Lisa *had never seen / had never been seeing* such a beautiful painting.
5 Amanda *had worked / had been working* as a waitress for three years before she became a singer.
6 By the time the film ended, she *had fallen / had been falling* asleep on the sofa.
7 What *had they seen / had they been seeing* that made them so frightened?
8 *Had you lived / Had you been living* in the house for long before the fire destroyed it?

3 **Complete the sentences with the past perfect simple or past perfect continuous form of the verbs.**

1 Mary _____ (study) for ten hours before she went to bed.
2 How long _____ (you / clean) your room for when your mother arrived yesterday?
3 I _____ (drive) for three hours when the accident happened.
4 She told the doctor that she _____ (not / sleep) for two nights.
5 Until I found this job, I _____ (search) for almost ten months without success.
6 Until yesterday, he _____ (never / ride) a motorbike before.
7 By the time I got to the theatre, the play _____ (start).
8 We still _____ (not / finish) cooking by the time our guests arrived.

4 **Choose the correct time expression (a–c) to complete the sentences.**

1 She had been waiting for an opportunity like this ___ years.
  a for   b since   c already

2 What exactly had they been doing ___ ?
  a today   b all day   c next time

3 Mark had never been to a Formula 1 race ___ .
  a after   b just   c before

4 ___ I had spoken, I regretted it.
  a As soon as   b While   c Until

5 ___ had you been practising for?
  a What time   b How long   c When

6 We had ___ met two years before, and I had asked for his advice.
  a never   b always   c already

5 **Complete the sentences with one word in each gap.**

1 By the _____ I was 11, I'd learned to play five different musical instruments.
2 We hadn't been on holiday _____ a very long time.
3 Tina had _____ training all afternoon and now she felt tired.
4 _____ you looked under the bed for your laptop before you asked to borrow Simon's?
5 It was a disappointing match. We had been looking forward to it _____ season.
6 She had done a lot of research _____ she interviewed the professor.
7 No, we had _____ heard of the actor – that's why we didn't know he was famous.
8 _____ had they done to win first prize in the competition?

6 Write questions for the answers.

1 A: _____ ?
   B: I'd been trying to get in touch with her for three months.

2 A: _____ ?
   B: Yes, he had been told about the new deadline.

3 A: _____ ?
   B: She had tried on three pairs of shoes before she found a pair she liked.

4 A: _____ ?
   B: I had been working in the garden.

5 A: _____ ?
   B: No, he hadn't been crying. He'd been sleeping.

6 A: _____ ?
   B: I'd met her twice before.

7 A: _____ ?
   B: She had spoken to him the day before yesterday.

8 A: _____ ?
   B: They had just been to the circus.

7 Correct the sentences where necessary. Tick those which do not need correcting.

1 I hadn't sold any paintings since ages.

   _____

2 Maria had been dancing with Paulo all night.

   _____

3 Mum was upset because the twins had been fight again.

   _____

4 How long had it been for you had checked your emails?

   _____

5 Had they been practise for the concert for a long time?

   _____

6 We voted after everyone has had the chance to give their opinion.

   _____

Vocabulary

Phrasal verbs

8 Match the phrasal verbs (1–8) with their meanings (a–h).

1	catch on	☐	a	be as good as
2	catch up on	☐	b	become popular
3	come in for	☐	c	not be punished for doing something wrong
4	come up with	☐	d	(of time) pass
5	get away with	☐	e	circulate or spread
6	go around	☐	f	receive (criticism or praise)
7	go by	☐	g	suggest an idea or plan
8	live up to	☐	h	find out what's been happening

9 Complete the sentences with the correct form of the phrasal verbs from Exercise 8.

1 There is a rumour _____ that a famous athlete is visiting our school.

2 Tom is reading the paper to _____ all the latest news.

3 The photographer _____ a lot of criticism for his last exhibition.

4 Ella has _____ a brilliant idea to help the local community.

5 Do you think that meeting a celebrity would _____ your expectations?

6 The new style of trainers wasn't very comfortable, so it never really _____ .

7 People who cheat in exams should never _____ it.

8 I can't believe that two whole weeks have _____ and there hasn't been any rain!

Prepositions

10 Choose the correct option to complete the sentences.

1 Have you ever made a fool of yourself *at / in / by / behind* public?

2 The audience seldom know what goes on *at / in / by / behind* the scenes of a theatre.

3 Success always comes *at / in / by / behind* a price – and that price is usually years of hard work.

4 She hopes to follow *at / in / by / behind* her aunt's footsteps and become an architect.

5 Can I talk to you *at / in / by / behind* private? I have something important to tell you.

6 *At / In / By / Behind* all accounts, this is the best film she has ever made.

Collocations and expressions

11 Complete the sentences with the correct form of these words.

| draw | lead | lose | see | seize | set |

1 I love science. I don't think I will ever _____ my passion for it.

2 Malala Yousafzai has _____ the way in fighting for the rights of girls to education.

3 Famous sports people should _____ a good example by playing fairly.

4 When Dan had a holiday job at the theatre, he _____ the chance to talk to the actors.

5 We played a joke on Dad, but he didn't _____ the funny side of it!

6 Some celebrities don't like to _____ attention to themselves in public.

Words easily confused

12 Complete the sentences with the correct form of these words. Use each word at least once.

1 | gap | interval | pause |

a The dog must have escaped through a(n) _____ in the fence.

b The play was so bad that we left during the _____ .

c There are _____ in the online lesson which give you time to practise.

2 | borrow | hire | lend | rent |

a Harold denied that I had _____ him the money.

b We've _____ a villa for the whole summer.

c If I were you, I wouldn't _____ money from anyone.

d They _____ a children's entertainer for the party.

3 | amount | extent | range |

a You can choose from a wide _____ of books at this shop.

b I agree with you to some _____ , but we differ on a few points.

c They received a large _____ of money to build a new concert hall.

4 | memorise   recognise   remember   remind |

   a He'd changed so much that I didn't _____ him.

   b _____ to switch off the lights when you leave.

   c The actors spent a long time trying to _____ their lines for the play.

   d _____ me to phone Grandad this evening.

Word formation   verb → noun

13 **Use the word in capitals to form a word that fits in the gap.**

   1 It can take a long time and a lot of work to make your dreams a _____ .   **REALISE**

   2 I've never forgotten the _____ that my piano teacher gave me.   **ENCOURAGE**

   3 The painter took many _____ from other artists to create his style.   **INFLUENCE**

   4 The airline is one of the football team's biggest _____ .   **SPONSOR**

   5 Remember that _____ can be an important part of the learning process.   **FAIL**

   6 Very few writers achieve _____ with their first book.   **SUCCEED**

   7 What was the _____ for the band's new album?   **INSPIRE**

   8 You need a lot of _____ to find your dream job.   **DETERMINE**

Sentence transformation

14 **Complete the second sentence so that it has a similar meaning to the first sentence, using the word given. Do not change the word given. You must use between two and five words.**

   1 Mary didn't start eating until all the family had sat down.

     BEFORE

     Mary waited until all the family _____ she started eating.

   2 When we got home, she was still painting the room.

     FINISHED

     She _____ the room when we arrived.

   3 Natalie graduated from university, then travelled around the world.

     AFTER

     Natalie travelled around the world _____ from university.

   4 Serena had some interesting ideas for our project.

     UP

     Serena _____ some interesting ideas for our project.

   5 Lots of people praised Mark's essay in the school magazine.

     CAME

     Mark's essay in the school magazine _____ a lot of praise.

   6 The presentation was interesting, so it felt like the time passed quickly.

     BY

     The time seemed to _____ quickly because the presentation was interesting.

   7 Everybody says this is a terrible novel.

     ACCOUNTS

     By _____ , this is a terrible novel.

   8 The musician wore dark glasses because he didn't want people to see him.

     DRAW

     The musician wore dark glasses because he didn't want to _____ himself.

Awareness

1 **Which of these sentences are correct (C) and incorrect (I)?**

1 Dan was in bed for an hour when we got home. ___

2 We never found out what had happened. ___

3 By the time he was 14 he had since become rich. ___

4 Had the audience stopped clapping when you left the stage? ___

5 They were starving because they hadn't had breakfast. ___

6 Did you been waiting long? ___

7 I was annoyed because I had worked hard on the project. ___

8 Someone had drink all the milk. ___

9 We hadn't been driving long when we got a puncture. ___

10 They had woke in the night to find their tent had been stolen. ___

How many did you get right? ☐

Grammar

Past simple, past perfect simple and past perfect continuous

When we want to show in which order actions happened in the past, we use the past perfect for the action that happened first in the past and we use the past simple for the actions that followed.
He **had been working** as a mechanic when a football agent **discovered** him and signed him to Manchester City. (First, he had been working as a mechanic and then a football agent discovered him.)

In time clauses with words like *after, as soon as, before, by the time, once, until* and *when*, you can use either the past simple or the past perfect to refer to an earlier event, with no important difference in meaning.
As soon as I (had) finished my homework, I went out.
I went out as soon as I (had) finished my homework.

Grammar exercises

2 **Choose the correct option to complete the sentences.**

1 When I *saw / had seen* Bill yesterday, he hadn't sold his car.

2 The plane *already took off / had already taken off* when we arrived at the airport.

3 As soon as she got home, she realised that somebody *broke / had broken* in and stolen all her medals.

4 When I *arrived / had arrived* at the cinema, my friend Alice had already bought the tickets.

5 After I *ran / had been running* for an hour, I stopped to have a drink.

6 By the time Zak *phoned / had phoned* Amelia, she had already arranged to go out.

7 That was the first time I *ever sang / had ever sung* on stage.

8 The moment the bus arrived, I realised that I *left / had left* my wallet at home.

3 **Complete the sentences with one word in each gap.**

1 We _____ not feel like going out the other night.

2 By the time the photographer arrived, the guests _____ left.

3 David and Megan had only _____ playing in the band for a few weeks.

4 _____ Greta have enough time to practise before the competition?

5 Where _____ they met before?

6 I didn't want to leave _____ I had shown everyone my certificate.

7 She hadn't performed on stage _____ her last year at school.

8 We had been _____ a lovely time when we realised that we were at the wrong party.

4 Complete the sentences with the past simple, past perfect simple or past perfect continuous form of the verbs.

1 The teacher _____ (tell) us that he _____ (teach) for ten years.

2 She _____ (try) to explain how she _____ (come up with) her invention.

3 By the time I _____ (get) to the concert hall, the choir _____ (sing) for over half an hour.

4 I _____ (not / relax) until I _____ (finish) my presentation.

5 We _____ (look) for a hotel room since we _____ (arrive) in the city, and we were exhausted.

6 John _____ (not / ride) very long when he _____ (realise) that he _____ (forget) to bring his packed lunch.

7 How long _____ (you / walk) in the mountains when it _____ (start) to rain?

8 _____ (you / see) the children when they _____ (get) home last night? They _____ (be) very dirty and really tired! What _____ (they / do)?

5 Complete the sentences with these time expressions.

| after   already   by the time   for   since   until |

1 I only started taking driving lessons _____ I had bought a new car.

2 The train had already left _____ we reached the station.

3 Susanna had been waiting for me _____ four o'clock.

4 They had been trying to solve the problem _____ three hours when they finally found the solution.

5 She had _____ done her homework by the time her friend came to see her.

6 He didn't leave _____ he had paid the bill.

6 Use the prompts to write sentences with the past simple and past perfect.

1 Sally / not / finish writing her essay / when / I call her

_____

2 As soon as / I finish the race / I realise / I run my fastest time

_____

3 They / not / start the ceremony / until / all the guests arrive

_____

4 By the time / he be 25 / he / become a successful designer

_____

5 After / the famous actor / win an Oscar / she retire

_____

6 We / not / serve the cake / until / everyone / finish the main course

_____

7 Natalie / not graduate from university / when / they offer her a job

_____

8 I / finish / my homework / by the time / I go to bed

_____

7 Write questions for the answers.

1 A: _____ ?
   B: I finished my homework an hour ago.

2 A: _____ ?
   B: Yes, we'd been talking for quite a long time.

3 A: _____ ?
   B: They had been travelling around South America.

4 A: _____ ?
   B: No, I hadn't heard the song before.

5 A: _____ ?
   B: Yes, I thought it was a good idea at the time.

6 A: _____ ?
   B: They had been performing in small clubs and at parties.

7 A: _____ ?
   B: The journalist interviewed the writer last week.

8 A: _____ ?
   B: She was excited because she had just spoken to an astronaut.

Vocabulary

Phrasal verbs

8 Match the phrasal verbs (1–8) with their meanings (a–h).

1 live for   ☐   a begin

2 live on   ☐   b respect and admire

3 look down on   ☐   c investigate or examine

4 look into   ☐   d mainly eat a particular kind of food

5 look up to   ☐   e think you are better than someone else

6 make up for   ☐   f not have the opportunity to enjoy something

7 miss out on   ☐   g have something or someone as the most important thing in your life

8 start out   ☐   h when something good replaces something bad

9 Complete the sentences with the correct form of the phrasal verbs from Exercise 8.

1 The head teacher promised to _____ the accusations of cheating in his school.

2 She thinks she's so great. She _____ everyone!

3 No one should have to _____ an education.

4 I've always _____ my grandmother. She made an important discovery in chemistry.

5 Do you think that having money would _____ losing your privacy?

6 My uncle is a famous journalist who _____ at a local newspaper.

7 I love Italian food. I could _____ pasta very happily!

8 Sara is very passionate about music. In fact, you could say she _____ it.

Prepositions

10 Choose the correct option to complete the sentences.

1 I haven't been sleeping well because I've been *on / to / under / without* a lot of pressure.

2 He wasn't able to do PE that day *on / to / under / without* account of his bad leg.

3 Much *on / to / under / without* our astonishment, we won the match 6–1.

4 Don't worry, we have everything *on / to / under / without* control.

5 He couldn't make it to the ceremony, so his manager accepted the award *on / to / under / without* his behalf.

6 That was *on / to / under / without* a doubt the most terrifying rollercoaster ride I have ever been on.

Collocations and expressions

11 Complete the sentences with these words.

anywhere   doors   fame   name   nowhere   success

1 The band came out of _____ . A year ago, no one had heard of them.

2 If you don't practise the guitar regularly, you'll never get _____ with it.

3 Everyone knows the TV presenter now – she's a household _____ .

4 He's talented, but knowing a film producer certainly opened _____ for him.

5 The secret of my _____ is not being afraid to fail sometimes.

6 My sister's claim to _____ is that she won a national science competition when she was ten.

Words easily confused

12 Complete the sentences with the correct form of these words. Use each word at least once.

1 prescription   receipt   recipe   review

a You can't exchange goods without a _____ .

b The play received excellent _____ .

c I found the _____ for this meal on an app.

d You need a _____ to get this medicine.

2 charge   fee   payment   reward   tip

a I won't leave a _____ if I'm not satisfied with the service.

b A _____ has been offered for information leading to the return of the stolen medals.

c We deliver and install the system at no extra _____ .

d The _____ are so high that few parents can afford to send their children to that school.

e Unless we receive _____ within a week, your order will be cancelled.

3 company   factory   firm   industry

a She works for a law _____ in the capital.

b The inventor saw her idea being made into reality at the _____ .

c All the managers here have _____ cars.

d This area depends heavily on the film _____ .

4 disgrace   gossip   rumour   scandal

a There's a _____ going round that the singer is leaving the band.

b I'm not interested in celebrity _____ , so I don't read that magazine.

c Many people have called for the players to resign after the cheating _____ .

d The way the celebrity was treated by photographers was a _____ !

6

Word formation   noun → noun

13 Use the word in capitals to form a word that fits in the gap.

1 Sadly, our _____ ended when the band split up.   **FRIEND**
2 The world's leading _____ all agree that global warming is real.   **SCIENCE**
3 He left school at 16 and got a job in a _____ .   **BAKER**
4 Some famous journalists started out as _____ on the internet.   **BLOG**
5 In the oral test, the _____ will ask you questions about your life.   **EXAM**
6 Green eyes are a common _____ in our family.   **CHARACTER**
7 The time has come for _____ , not words.   **ACT**
8 I have only one _____ of the play – it was incredibly boring.   **CRITIC**
9 What _____ are you?   **NATION**
10 The football team receives a large amount of _____ from a mobile   **SPONSOR**
   phone company.

Sentence transformation

14 Complete the second sentence so that it has a similar meaning to the first sentence, using the word given. Do not change the word given. You must use between two and five words.

1 Dad didn't go to bed until my brother had come home.
   WAITED
   Dad _____ come home before he went to bed.

2 It was the first time our teacher had shouted at us.
   NEVER
   Our teacher _____ before.

3 Which famous people do you respect and admire?
   LOOK
   Which famous people do you _____ ?

4 Truly great people don't think they're better than other people.
   DOWN
   Truly great people don't _____ other people.

5 Football is the most important thing in Malcolm's life.
   FOR
   Malcolm _____ football.

6 Because of her illness, Stella couldn't go to the award ceremony.
   ACCOUNT
   Stella couldn't go to the award ceremony _____ her illness.

7 That was the best party this year, definitely.
   DOUBT
   That was _____ the best party this year.

8 The police are investigating the disappearance of the painting.
   INTO
   The police _____ the disappearance of the painting.

Unit 7

1 **Which of these sentences are correct (C) and incorrect (I)?**

1 I've decided I'm not going join the army. ___
2 Will you come this way, please? ___
3 We'll had left this place by the weekend. ___
4 Shall we going to a restaurant this evening? ___
5 By the time you'll get home, you'll be exhausted. ___

6 I think I'll get a taxi home tonight. ___
7 You'll have been working here since two years tomorrow. ___
8 Look out! That dog is going to bite you. ___
9 After I'm going to have a bath, I'm going out. ___
10 He'll be doing his final exam this time next week. ___

How many did you get right? [ ]

Grammar

will

Affirmative	Negative	Questions
I / He / She / It / We / You / They **will** drive.	I / He / She / It / We / You / They **will not (won't)** drive.	**Will** I / he / she / it / we / you / they drive?
Short answers		
Yes, I / he / she / it / we / you / they **will**.	**No**, I / he / she / it / we / you / they **won't**.	

We use *will*:
- for decisions made at the time of speaking.
*It's hot in here. I'**ll open** the window.*
- for predictions.
*Buses **won't have** drivers in the future.*
- for promises.
*I'**ll book** tickets tonight, I promise.*
- for threats.
*If you don't clear the table, I **won't take** you to the cinema.*
- to talk about future facts.
*The new game **will be released** in May.*
- after verbs like *think, believe, be sure, expect*, etc. and before words like *probably, maybe*, etc.
*I'm sure the new shopping centre **will be** popular.*
- to offer to do something for someone.
*I'**ll help** you with that.*
- to ask someone to do something.
***Will you make** me a sandwich, please?*

Note

We use *shall* with *I* and *we* in questions or when we want to make a suggestion or an offer.
*Where **shall we eat**?*
***Shall** we **have** lunch before the show?*
***Shall** I **park** the car on the street?*

We can use *should* instead of *will* to make a prediction when we're not 100% sure.
*Our guests **should be** here soon, I expect.*
*Don't worry – it **shouldn't be** a problem to get a refund.*

7

be going to

Affirmative	Negative	Questions
I am ('m) going to drive. He / She / It is ('s) going to drive. We / You / They are ('re) going to drive.	I am ('m) not going to drive. He / She / It is not (isn't) going to drive. We / You / They are not (aren't) going to drive.	Am I going to drive? Is he / she / it going to drive? Are we / you / they going to drive?
Short answers		
Yes, I am. Yes, he / she / it is. Yes, we / you / they are.	No, I'm not. No, he / she / it isn't. No, we / you / they aren't.	

We use *be going to* for:
- future plans.

Jane is going to buy an electric car.
- predictions for the near future based on present situations or evidence.

Look at the queue! It's going to take a long time to get a table.

Note

Some common time expressions that are often used with *will* and *be going to* are: *this week / month / summer, tonight, this evening, tomorrow, tomorrow morning / afternoon / night, next week / month / year, at the weekend, in April, in a few minutes / hours / days, on Tuesday, on Saturday morning,* etc.
I'll tell you all about the concert tonight.

Future continuous

Affirmative	Negative	Questions
I / He / She / It / We / You / They will be working.	I / He / She / It / We / You / They will not (won't) be working.	Will I / he / she / it / we / you / they be working?
Short answers		
Yes, I / he / she / it / we / you / they will.	No, I / he / she / it / we / you / they won't.	

Spelling: dance → dancing, travel → travelling, tidy → tidying

We use the future continuous for:
- actions in progress at a specific time in the future.

We'll be arriving at the airport at this time next week.
- plans and arrangements for the future.

Parents will be attending a meeting about the new school.

Note

Some common time expressions that are often used with the future continuous are: *this time next week / month / summer, this time tomorrow morning / afternoon / night,* etc.
This time tomorrow, he'll be working in the new office.

Future perfect simple and future perfect continuous

Affirmative	Negative	Questions
I / He / She / It / We / You / They will have worked / been working.	I / He / She / It / We / You / They will not (won't) have worked / been working.	Will I / he / she / it / we / you / they have worked / been working?
Short answers		
Yes, I / he / she / it / we / you / they will.	No, I / he / she / it / we / you / they won't.	

Spelling: walk → walked, dance → danced, travel → travelled, tidy → tidied, play → played

We use the future perfect simple to talk about:

- something that will be finished by or before a specific time in the future.

*The builders **will have finished** by the end of this week.*

- the length of time that an action will have lasted for at a point of time in the future.

*I'**ll have worked** here for three years next month.*

We use the future perfect continuous when we are looking back to the past from a point in the future. We can use it to talk about events or situations that will happen over a period of time and may have a result.

*By the end of tomorrow, I'**ll have been studying** all day, so I'll be tired.*

Time phrases

When we use time phrases such as *when, before, after, until, once, by the time,* etc. to talk about the future, we use them with a present or a present perfect tense. We do not use them with a future tense.

*After I **have been** shopping, I'll meet a friend for lunch.*
***By the time** he **gets** to work, he'll be soaking wet.*

We use the present perfect simple to emphasise that the first action must be finished before the second starts.

***Once** you **have bought** the ticket, you can go anywhere in the park.* (You need to buy the ticket and then you will be able to go anywhere in the park.)

> **Note**
>
> Some verbs are irregular and do not follow these spelling rules. See a list of irregular verbs and their past participles on pages 172–173.

> **Note**
>
> Other tenses that describe the future are the present simple for timetabled events, and the present continuous for plans and arrangements.
>
> *The train to Manchester **leaves** at three o'clock.*
> *My sister **is moving in** to her new flat next week.*

> **Note**
>
> Some common time phrases that are often used with the future perfect simple and continuous are: *by the end of the week / month / year, by this time tomorrow, by tomorrow morning / ten o'clock / 2023,* etc.

Grammar exercises

2 **Choose the correct option to complete the sentences.**

1 I promise *I'll never forget / I won't be forgetting* your birthday again.

2 *I'll work / I'll be working* at 9 p.m. – I won't be home at that time.

3 Wait a minute. *I'll call / I'll be calling* a taxi now.

4 Sue *will have been working / will work* here for ten years by the end of the month.

5 Dan *won't eat / won't have eaten,* so let's take him a sandwich.

6 Our friends *will be finishing / will have finished* eating by the time we arrive at the restaurant!

7 When I get home in the afternoon, my brother *will be playing / will play* basketball in the park.

8 Don't forget. The plane *lands / will land* at 7 p.m.

3 **Complete the sentences with *will* or the future continuous of the verbs.**

1 I _____ (help) you carry the sofa. Don't worry.

2 I think he _____ (be) here soon.

3 Don't call me at 6 p.m. – _____ (drive) home at that time.

4 This time tomorrow we _____ (have) lunch in the new restaurant.

5 I really don't know where _____ (work) this time next year.

6 It's an amazing building. I'm sure you _____ (like) it.

7

4 Complete the sentences with the *will* or *be going to* form of the verbs.

1 _____ (you / open) the door for me, please?

2 I've decided I _____ (buy) a flat.

3 Look at the red sky! It _____ (be) a nice day tomorrow.

4 Is your bike not working? I _____ (have) a look at it for you.

5 I promise I _____ (be) on time for the cinema this evening.

6 We _____ (play) tennis this evening. The court is booked for 6 p.m.

5 Complete the sentences with the future continuous, future perfect simple or future perfect continuous of the verbs.

1 By the end of next month, I _____ (sing) in the choir for ten years.

2 If Martin is with them, they _____ (talk) about architecture.

3 I _____ (work) late this evening, so don't wait up for me.

4 By the year 2030, we _____ (build) 100,000 new homes.

5 We _____ (stay) with my aunt until we find another flat.

6 At the end of the year, Dr Green _____ (teach) at this university for thirty years.

6 Choose the correct option (a–b).

1 Can you come shopping with us tomorrow morning?
   a Sorry, but I'll see my dentist tomorrow morning.
   b Sorry, but I'm seeing my dentist tomorrow morning.

2 I'd really like to meet you on Saturday.
   a Great! I'm not doing anything then.
   b Great! I don't do anything then.

3 What are you thinking about?
   a This time tomorrow, I will fly to New York.
   b This time tomorrow, I'll be flying to New York.

4 This is the second time you've lied to me.
   a Sorry, Mum. I'll never lie to you again.
   b Sorry, Mum. I won't be lying to you again.

5 Can you give Tom this parcel for me, please?
   a Of course I can. I will have seen Tom today.
   b Of course I can. I am seeing Tom today.

6 Are you reading another book?
   a Yes, I will be finishing it by this evening.
   b Yes, I will have finished it by this evening.

7 Complete the sentences with one word in each gap.

1 I'm going _____ do my maths homework now.

2 By noon, I will _____ painted my room blue.

3 Will you _____ attending the seminar this afternoon?

4 He's not _____ to finish this by six o'clock.

5 _____ Simon going to cycle this evening?

6 When _____ you have completed your design?

7 By the time the meal _____ ready, I'll be starving!

8 Sara will have _____ waiting for hours by now.

Vocabulary

Phrasal verbs

8 Match the phrasal verbs (1–8) with their meanings (a–h).

1	hang out	☐	**a** go on holiday or a break
2	hang up	☐	**b** spend time with somebody socially
3	hang on	☐	**c** change the subject you are talking about
4	move in	☐	**d** stop a telephone conversation
5	move out	☐	**e** start living in a place
6	move on	☐	**f** start feeling comfortable in a place
7	settle down	☐	**g** wait for a short while
8	get away	☐	**h** leave the place you live in

9 Complete the sentences with the correct form of the phrasal verbs from Exercise 8.

1 We _____ of our flat when my little brother was born.
2 Please _____ a minute. I'll see if I can find your order.
3 It took us a while to _____ in our new house, but we really love it now.
4 The Ross family like to try to _____ to the countryside twice a year.
5 He's going to redecorate before he _____ to his new place.
6 Terry is _____ with his friends at the shopping centre.
7 Let's _____ to another subject, shall we?
8 Samantha _____ the phone before we had finished talking!

Prepositions

10 Choose the correct option to complete the sentences.

1 One of the advantages *of / among / on* living in the city is that everything you need is nearby.
2 We agreed to buy the house *of / among / on* condition that they lowered the price.
3 London is *of / among / on* the most expensive cities in the world to live in.
4 Sammy got the job as a result *of / among / on* his qualifications and experience.
5 We get our post delivered to us *of / among / on* a daily basis.
6 We didn't like the flat because, *of / among / on* other things, it didn't have any windows.

Collocations and expressions

11 Complete the sentences with the correct form of these words.

consideration   ghost   place   talk   town   world

1 These directions aren't very clear. They're all over the _____ !
2 This town is becoming like a _____ town. Bands don't play here anymore.
3 I've got the best of both _____ – I live in the city, but near a huge park.
4 Tom and Kate really went to _____ on their wedding. They spent a lot of money.
5 Her new exhibition is the _____ of the town.
6 The architect took the views of the local residents into _____ .

7

Words easily confused

12 Complete the sentences with the correct form of these words. Use each word at least once.

1 annoy   disturb   matter   mind   object

  a It doesn't _____ what you wear to the party.

  b What really _____ me is people walking slowly while they look at their phones.

  c I don't want to be _____ . Please leave me alone.

  d Dan _____ to anyone parking in front of his house.

  e Would you _____ helping me with the luggage?

2 attendance   attention   care   notice

  a Jill attracted the waiter's _____ by waving.

  b The students took no _____ of the 'No swimming' signs and dived into the lake.

  c Please pay _____ to what I'm saying.

  d These boxes must be handled with _____ .

  e Your _____ record in this class is very poor.

3 approval   attitude   opinion   view

  a From my point of _____ , it's a waste of time.

  b What provoked their hostile _____ towards you?

  c My boss showed her _____ of the way I ran the office by giving me a pay rise.

  d What's your _____ of the new process?

4 alike   identical   same   similar

  a It doesn't matter which way you go – the distance is _____ by either route.

  b The new shop sells the _____ types of clothes as the old shop.

  c They get on well together because they're so much _____ .

  d Your house is _____ to mine, but yours has a bigger garden.

Word formation   adjective → opposite adjective

13 Use the word in capitals to form a word that fits in the gap.

  1 We didn't tip the waiter because he was very _____ . **POLITE**

  2 It is very _____ that they'll move to the countryside – they love the city. **LIKELY**

  3 You can wear what you like at our office – we are very _____ . **FORMAL**

  4 Don't drive past the red traffic light – that's _____ ! **LEGAL**

  5 He's so _____ that I don't think he has ever told the truth in his life! **HONEST**

  6 It was really _____ of you to let Dan borrow your car – he hasn't got a licence! **RESPONSIBLE**

  7 I'm afraid my new hairstyle makes me look rather _____ . **ATTRACTIVE**

  8 Your office is very _____ . I'm surprised you ever find anything! **ORGANISED**

  9 What a(n) _____ film that was. Incredible! **ORDINARY**

  10 The shop is open at such _____ times – we never know when we can go there. **REGULAR**

Sentence transformation

14 Complete the second sentence so that it has a similar meaning to the first sentence, using the word given. Do not change the word given. You must use between two and five words.

1 Our party is on Saturday afternoon at our house.
HAVING
We _____ our house on Saturday afternoon.

2 If you don't hurry, we'll arrive after the film starts.
STARTED
If you don't hurry, _____ by the time we arrive.

3 I started building the wall on Monday, and it's now Wednesday.
HAVE
By Thursday, I _____ the wall for four days.

4 We never really began to feel comfortable in the village.
SETTLED
We never really _____ in the village.

5 They like to go on holiday every winter.
AWAY
They like to _____ every winter.

6 Because of the roadworks, we had to go a different way.
ACCOUNT
We had to go a different way _____ the roadworks.

7 Who do you like to spend time with socially?
HANG
Who do you _____ with?

8 If you don't like your flatmates, you should leave the flat.
OUT
You should _____ if you don't like your flatmates.

1 Which of these sentences are correct (C) and incorrect (I)?

1 Take the rubbishes outside, please. ___
2 There is some good news for you in this letter. ___
3 Hurry up! We don't have many time. ___
4 The police were asking questions about Carol. ___
5 We're still waiting for some new equipments. ___

6 He gave me a useful advice. ___
7 How much brothers do you have? ___
8 Few people go to the theatre these days. ___
9 Can you give me an information, please? ___
10 He didn't invite many friends to the party. ___

How many did you get right? ☐

Grammar

Countable nouns

Most nouns are countable and have singular and plural forms.

shop → shops	lorry → lorries	boy → boys	potato → potatoes
beach → beaches	leaf → leaves	woman → women	foot → feet

We often use *a* or *an* with singular countable nouns.
a road   an avenue

We can use *some*, *any* or a number (for example, *three*) with plural countable nouns.
*There are **some** dogs in the park.*
*Are there **any** trees in your garden?*
*I haven't been to the cinema for **three** years.*

We can use singular or plural verb forms with countable nouns depending on whether we are talking about one item or more.
*A **bike** is useful when you live in a big city.*
***Lorries** are noisy and cause a lot of congestion.*

Remember

Some plural countable nouns don't end in *-s*. Remember to use a plural verb form with them.
*He ran for miles and now his **feet are** sore.*

Uncountable nouns

Some nouns are uncountable. They do not have plural forms.

advice	food	health	knowledge	music	time
biology	fruit	history	luggage	progress	traffic
chocolate	fun	homework	medicine	research	water
furniture	information	money	rubbish	weather	

We don't use *a* or *an* with uncountable nouns. We can use *some* and *any*.
*I'd like **some** food, please.*   *I haven't got **any** money with me.*

We always use singular verb forms with uncountable nouns.
***Is** this information correct?*   *The traffic **was** awful!*

Remember

Some uncountable nouns end in *-s*. Remember to use a singular verb form with them.
*The **news** this morning was shocking.*   ***Maths is** my favourite subject.*

Nouns that can be countable or uncountable

Many nouns can be either countable or uncountable. Sometimes there is only a small difference in meaning.
*Would you like **some tea**? (uncountable)*   *Would you like **a tea**? (countable, a cup of tea)*

Sometimes there is a very different meaning.

Countable	Uncountable
The new meeting **room** is very comfortable.	Is there any more **room** on the bus?
The car park was full. There were no **spaces**.	There isn't enough **space** in this office!

Nouns that are always plural

Some nouns are never used in the singular form (with a particular meaning) and always take a plural verb.
*I didn't like the **clothes** in the shop window.*
*I can't read that sign. I think I might need **glasses**.*
*The **police** were talking to people in the street.*

Quantifiers

We use *some* with both uncountable and plural countable nouns in affirmative sentences and in requests or offers.
*I bought **some headphones** this weekend.*
*Could I have **some advice**, please?*
*Would you like **some help** to carry those?*

We use *any* with both uncountable and plural countable nouns in negative sentences and in questions.
*There isn't **any furniture** in the apartment.*
*Have you seen **any** good **films** lately?*

We use *a lot of / lots of* with both uncountable and plural countable nouns.
***Lots of people** visited the exhibition.*
*There was **a lot of rubbish** in the park.*

We use *(a) little* (or *a bit of*) with uncountable nouns and *(a) few* with plural countable nouns in affirmative sentences. We use *a little / a few* to emphasise that there is a positive amount (i.e. more than zero). We use *little / few* to emphasise a negative amount (i.e. not as much / many as expected).
*We've done **a little** research already. (= more than none)*
*There is **little** research on the subject. (= not enough)*
***A few** residents came to look at the plans. (= a reasonable number)*
***Few** residents wanted a new motorway. (= hardly any)*

We use *much* with uncountable nouns and *many* with plural countable nouns in negative sentences and in questions.
*How **much** luggage are you taking?*
*There aren't **many** students in this part of the city.*

We can use *as much / many as* to talk about a surprisingly large number.
***As many as** 80,000 people watched the match in the stadium.*

all, whole, every and *each*

Every and *each* always take a singular noun. *Every* suggests a larger number, but both words are often possible.
***Each / Every** house in the street has its own garden.*
When we use *all* with a singular countable noun, it means 'from beginning to end'.
*I worked **all** day on Saturday. (= from morning to evening)*
Whole has a similar meaning, but it's an adjective, not a quantifier, so it usually comes after *a / the*.
*I worked **the whole** day.*

Quantifiers with and without *of*

After some quantifiers, we add *of* before a noun.
a lot of commuters, **plenty of** light, *a bit of* space, etc.
After some quantifiers, we don't normally add *of* before a noun.
several people, *a little* time, **most** people, etc.
However, we need to add *of* before *the*, a possessive (e.g. *my*) or a pronoun (e.g. *us*).
*several **of the** people, a little **of my** time, most **of them***
We can usually omit *of* after *all* and *both*, with no change of meaning.
all (of) the traffic, both (of) my shoes

8

Grammar exercises

2 **Complete the sentences with the plural form of the nouns.**

1 There were some intelligent _____ at the meeting. (woman)

2 The archeologists made some interesting _____ . (discovery)

3 The shop had a display of _____ in the window. (toy)

4 James couldn't reach the top three _____ of the bookcase. (shelf)

5 The rose _____ in her garden looked beautiful. (bush)

6 Could you go to the market and buy six _____ , please? (tomato)

7 The _____ of the city from the air were amazing. (photo)

8 If your _____ are hurting, you should see a dentist. (tooth)

3 **Decide if these nouns countable or uncountable. Complete the table.**

| boy | city | citizen | countryside | damage | furniture | leaf | potato |
| progress | research | shelf | street | stress | traffic | tree | weather |

Countable				
Uncountable				

4 **Complete the sentences with *a*, *an*, *some* or *any*.**

1 We would like _____ information about the rooms in your hotel.

2 Mum, I need _____ money to buy _____ new notebook.

3 I watched _____ unusual film at the cinema yesterday.

4 We haven't bought _____ new furniture for years!

5 I'll get you _____ coffee. Would you like milk and sugar with it?

6 No, thank you. We don't need _____ advertising at the moment.

5 **Complete the sentences with *few*, *a few*, *little*, *a little* or *a lot*.**

1 _____ people applied for the job, so they put another advertisement on the website.

2 The village is in a beautiful area, with very _____ pollution.

3 Jack has _____ of friends in this town. It seems that everybody likes him.

4 I gave my teacher _____ ideas for the class project. He liked them a lot.

5 In _____ years, most people will be using electric cars.

6 I have _____ free time today. How about going to the cinema?

7 'Mum, I need _____ of help to fix my bike,' said Lauren.

8 The cyclist had _____ patience with the driver who was rude to him.

6 **Write questions using *How much* or *How many*.**

1 A: _____ ? B: I've been to France twice.

2 A: _____ ? B: I have £16.

3 A: _____ ? B: It's three days to my birthday.

4 A: _____ ? B: There were 20 people at my party.

5 A: _____ ? B: It takes a lot of time to learn the piano.

6 A: _____ ? B: We just need a little milk.

7 Choose the correct option to complete the sentences.

1 My friend and I go running for an hour *all / every* Saturday.
2 *Each / Whole* house in the street is painted a different colour.
3 The planners spent the *whole / all* afternoon in a meeting.
4 *All / Each* competitor has an individual number.
5 Sam has cycled to school *every / whole* day this week.
6 I waited *whole / all* day for the new furniture to arrive.
7 The journalist said that the council was spending as *much / many* as £5 million on the project.
8 The organisers say they expect as *much / many* as 20,000 people to attend the festival.

8 Complete the sentences with one word in each gap.

1 Can I have a few _____ your peanuts, please?
2 There are _____ fresh yoghurts in the fridge.
3 No, thank you. I don't want _____ money.
4 I'm afraid the news _____ not good.
5 There aren't _____ places to play in this town – just a park and the village hall.
6 _____ of students live in this part of the city.
7 The traffic _____ really bad this morning.
8 My feet _____ hurting quite badly at the moment.

Vocabulary

Phrasal verbs

9 Match the phrasal verbs (1–8) with their meanings (a–h).

1 get across	☐	a	have a good relationship with
2 get at	☐	b	stand up
3 get round to	☐	c	finally do something which you meant to do
4 get in	☐	d	be chosen or accepted into an institution
5 get on	☐	e	succeed in making someone understand something
6 get out of	☐	f	succeed in a competition or exam
7 get through	☐	g	avoid doing something which you don't want to do
8 get up	☐	h	be able to reach something

10 Complete the sentences with the correct form of the phrasal verbs from Exercise 9.

1 It is important to _____ with your colleagues.
2 I've got lots of homework, and I must _____ doing it before the weekend.
3 Our team _____ the second round of the competition, then we were beaten 4–0.
4 Everyone _____ out of their seats and applauded when he walked onto the stage.
5 Put the biscuits on the top shelf, so that the dog can't _____ them.
6 The message I am trying to _____ is 'be safe'.
7 Sam was very happy when he _____ to his first choice of university.
8 If I can _____ going into town, I will. I really don't feel like it.

8

Prepositions

11 Choose the correct option to complete the sentences.

1 You can do what you like this weekend *as / for / in* far as I'm concerned.

2 I'm just going to sit here and relax *as / for / in* the moment – then I'll start work.

3 It wasn't such a bad film – *as / for / in* a matter of fact, I really enjoyed it.

4 They used to meet *as / for / in* secret in the park after school.

5 Why don't we go somewhere else *as / for / in* a change?

6 You need to submit your application *as / for / in* writing.

Collocations and expressions

12 Complete the sentences with these words.

> fail   increase   jungle   lane   life   temptation

1 I can never resist the _____ to buy fresh bread from the bakery.

2 The city is sometimes referred to as an urban _____ .

3 Do you like living life in the fast _____ ?

4 This train is never late. It arrives at 7.43 every day, without _____ .

5 My parents came from very different walks of _____ .

6 The number of people cycling to work is on the _____ . It went up by 12% last year.

Words easily confused

13 Complete the sentences with the correct form of these words. Use each word at least once.

1 > lay   lie   scatter   spread

  a The demonstrators _____ when the riot police appeared.

  b On average, our hens _____ one egg a day.

  c The detectives _____ out and searched the field for clues.

  d Could you help me _____ the table, please?

  e _____ down if you feel tired and need to rest.

2 > age   period   term   time

  a In this day and _____ , up-to-date information is vital.

  b We get our school reports at the end of _____ .

  c Do you remember the _____ when we got lost in Rome?

  d He spent a long _____ of his life working in China.

3 > condition   position   situation   state

  a We've bought a second-hand car in excellent _____ .

  b The _____ got worse and worse until war broke out a year later.

  c Finding herself in a _____ of power has changed her completely.

  d Your children are in an excellent _____ of health.

4 > damage   harm   injury   pain   wound

  a He still bears the scars of a _____ on his right leg.

  b A serious back _____ forced him to miss most of last season.

  c Brenda was in quite a lot of _____ after the operation.

  d Fortunately, the storm did little _____ to our property.

  e A short walk round the park won't do you any _____ !

Word formation   adverbs

14 Use the word in capitals to form a word that fits in the gap.

1 When everyone is sitting _____ , I will begin. **COMFORT**

2 If you are not aware of what you are doing, you are acting _____ . **CONSCIOUS**

3 People who speak _____ are never very popular. **OFFEND**

4 The economy is _____ getting stronger every year. **STEADY**

5 It was _____ kind of him to let you stay in his house. **EXTRAORDINARY**

6 I don't _____ agree with what she says, but she is making sense today. **GENERAL**

7 Peter drives so _____ that nobody will get in the car with him. **DANGER**

8 The light comes on _____ when someone enters the room. **AUTOMATIC**

9 If you didn't work so _____ , you wouldn't make so many mistakes. **CARE**

10 The director made the actors rehearse the scene _____ until it **REPEAT**
was perfect.

Sentence transformation

15 Complete the second sentence so that it has a similar meaning to the first sentence, using the word given. Do not change the word given. You must use between two and five words.

1 Not many students went on the school trip last week.

FEW

There was a school trip last week, but _____ went.

2 We have very little money, so we must spend carefully.

MUCH

We _____ money, so we must spend carefully.

3 Simon has very few friends in this school.

MANY

Simon _____ friends in this school.

4 I tried, but I couldn't make him understand my concerns.

ACROSS

I tried, but I couldn't _____ to him.

5 It is impossible to avoid the end-of-term exam.

GET

You can't _____ the end-of-term exam.

6 My sister and I have a really good relationship.

WELL

My sister and I _____ with each other.

7 I don't mind mind if they pay me at the end of the month.

CONCERNED

As _____ , they can pay me at the end of the month.

8 He asked me to write it down.

PUT

He asked me _____ writing.

Part 1

For questions 1–8, read the text below and decide which answer (A, B, C or D) best fits each gap. There is an example at the beginning (0).

Recycling in the office

One of the most exciting **(0)** ___ in the field of recycling is a machine that can clean used photocopier paper. The device, **(1)** ___ a decopier, uses a mixture of chemicals and a brush, and leaves the paper completely clean. **(2)** ___ to the manufacturers, the machine is **(3)** ___ of cleaning one sheet of paper at least five times. This is because the damage **(4)** ___ to the paper by the cleaning chemicals is compensated for by a special chemical which increases its strength.

It is predicted that the machine will **(5)** ___ on despite the high cost. The initial price of £30,000 will be too high for small companies, but they will be able to **(6)** ___ one for a reasonable monthly sum, or wait for a cheaper version to come out. Multinational companies will have a golden **(7)** ___ to help the environment and save money. What is more, the machine will, to a great **(8)** ___ , provide a way to improve security, as it offers an alternative to shredding confidential documents.

0	A	revelations	(B)	inventions	C	discoveries	D	concoctions
1	A	called	B	named	C	known	D	described
2	A	Listening	B	Speaking	C	Accounting	D	According
3	A	capable	B	able	C	possible	D	potential
4	A	made	B	exposed	C	inflicted	D	done
5	A	catch	B	get	C	carry	D	bring
6	A	take	B	lend	C	rent	D	borrow
7	A	chance	B	opportunity	C	occasion	D	possibility
8	A	length	B	extent	C	range	D	amount

Part 2

For questions 9–16, read the text below and think of the word which best fits each gap. Use only one word in each gap. There is an example at the beginning (0).

A commute with a view

At 3,650 metres above sea level, La Paz, in Bolivia, is **(0)** _____the_____ highest capital city in the world. Spread **(9)** _____ over the sides of a deep valley, it combines spacious residential areas, a modern commercial centre and overcrowded areas with people living on **(10)** _____ of each other in narrow streets and traditional houses.

La Paz is also home to the world's largest **(11)** _____ highest urban public transport system. However, this does not consist **(12)** _____ buses or trains, as you might expect, but cable cars. Opened **(13)** _____ 2014, the network links the commercial centre of La Paz with the neighbouring city of El Alto, **(14)** _____ is one of Bolivia's most rapidly-growing cities as people migrate from rural areas in search of employment.

The cable car network, known **(15)** _____ 'Mi Teleférico' ('my cable car') has changed the lives of the inhabitants of El Alto who work in La Paz, as many do. Daily commutes which **(16)** _____ to take two or three hours each way can now take half as long, or even less. And the view is certainly better!

Part 3

For questions 17–24, read the text below. Use the word given in capitals at the end of some of the lines to form a word that fits in the gap in the same line. There is an example at the beginning (0).

A better place to live

An Italian animal charity recently carried out a very **(0)** _____successful_____ operation. **SUCCESS**

They managed to transfer five unhappy tigers from an extremely small and **(17)** _____ **COMFORT**

cage in Italy to much more **(18)** _____ surroundings in England. This is just one of **LUXURY**

several wonderful examples of **(19)** _____ cooperation between animal welfare **NATIONAL**

organisations. The tigers' arrival at their new home has brought hope to people whose lives are

dedicated to the prevention of **(20)** _____ to animals on a daily basis. **CRUEL**

Of course, such happy endings are not always possible. **(21)** _____ , not all animals **FORTUNATE**

can be liberated from the often desperately **(22)** _____ conditions in which they are **HEALTH**

discovered. There are many reasons for this, but the most common one is delays in legal

procedures within the animals' host country.

Added to this is the fact that many courts are **(23)** _____ to the needs of animals **SENSE**

in captivity. Concern for animal welfare is not the same across different cultures. In order to end

this **(24)** _____ suffering, a greater understanding of the problem must be promoted **NECESSITY**

worldwide.

Part 4

For questions 25–30, complete the second sentence so that it has a similar meaning to the first sentence, using the word given. Do not change the word given. You must use between two and five words, including the word given. Here is an example (0).

Example:

0 She has always admired and respected her older sister.

LOOKED

She has always _____*looked up to*_____ her older sister.

25 The rent was lower than I had expected.

AS

The rent _____ I had expected.

26 This is her first chess tournament.

NEVER

She _____ chess tournament before.

27 I've never looked after a dog before.

USED

I _____ after a dog.

28 His answer to the first question was wrong.

MISTAKE

He _____ in the first question.

29 Karen will never let you pay her share of the bill.

INSISTS

Karen _____ her share of the bill.

30 Tim has suggested a brilliant idea for a holiday!

COME

Tim has _____ a brilliant idea for a holiday!

B2 Practice: ECCE

Grammar

For questions 1–20, choose the word or phrase that best completes the sentence or conversation.

1 When we arrived, the band ___ home.
   A had already went
   B have already went
   C had already gone
   D have already gone

2 They had been waiting ___ five hours.
   A since
   B until
   C yet
   D for

3 She ___ my letter by now.
   A receives
   B will have received
   C will be receiving
   D will receive

4 We'd finished by the ___ they got here.
   A hour
   B minute
   C time
   D second

5 ___ you close the window for me, please?
   A Are
   B Do
   C Will
   D Shall

6 She had never tried octopus ___ that day.
   A before
   B for
   C at
   D when

7 It ___ the first time she had driven a fast car.
   A was
   B is
   C had been
   D did

8 Does the soup need ___ more salt?
   A a little
   B a few
   C many
   D a lot of

9 Shall we just try and calm down ___ a moment?
   A for
   B at
   C with
   D by

10 '___ we go out tonight?'
   'Yes, let's.'
   A Are
   B Shall
   C Have
   D Do

11 After I ___ lunch, I'm going to bed.
   A will have
   B am having
   C have
   D had

12 I'd like ___ cheese and biscuits, please.
   A any
   B few
   C some
   D much

13 ___ you been informed about the meeting before it happened?
   A Have
   B Did
   C Had
   D Will

14 What are you ___ to study at university?
   A want
   B will
   C having
   D going

15 I was late because someone had ___ my keys.
   A hid
   B hidden
   C hiding
   D hide

16 You ___ left by the time I arrive, won't you?
   A will
   B have
   C going to
   D will have

17 Mum ___ at Grandma's house yet.
   A don't arrive
   B won't arrive
   C won't have arrived
   D hadn't arrived

18 Not too ___ cake for me, thanks.
   A many
   B lots
   C much
   D few

19 What ___ to win first prize in the competition?
   A had they done
   B did they
   C will they have done
   D do they

20 Sorry, but I haven't got ___ cash.
   A no
   B none
   C some
   D any

REVIEW 2

Vocabulary

For questions 21–40, choose the word or phrase that most appropriately completes the sentence.

21 I'll ___ into the possibility of forming a coding club.
A see
B hide
C watch
D look

22 How can I ___ up for forgetting your birthday?
A live
B make
C give
D come

23 I still haven't got ___ to writing to my mother.
A over
B round
C up
D through

24 That was delicious! Can I have the ___ ?
A receipt
B review
C recipe
D prescription

25 It's a nice idea, but I don't think it will ___ on.
A take
B have
C catch
D bring

26 As a ___ of fact, I do care about you.
A thing
B matter
C figure
D concept

27 Please ___ on a minute – I need to finish this call.
A wait
B hang
C move
D stay

28 Why does he look ___ on people?
A up
B over
C down
D round

29 George has become a household ___ since he acted in a TV series.
A face
B name
C man
D title

30 Koala bears ___ on eucalyptus leaves.
A eat
B drink
C are
D live

31 His latest novel ___ in for a lot of harsh criticism.
A came
B went
C ran
D fell

32 I'm catching ___ with my cousin on Saturday.
A down
B up
C along
D on

33 As far as I'm ___ , he can do what he wants.
A cared
B concerned
C known
D bothered

34 Greg has been ___ a lot of pressure.
A on
B at
C under
D over

35 The meeting was held ___ private.
A to
B on
C under
D in

36 It's a great restaurant, by all ___ .
A stories
B sayings
C bills
D accounts

37 Let's ___ somewhere for the weekend.
A get away
B go along
C get around
D go over

38 Shall we cycle into town, ___ a change?
A from
B for
C by
D in

39 I didn't understand the point he was trying to get ___ to us.
A in
B on
C across
D at

40 They really went to ___ on the food for the party!
A town
B world
C place
D zone

Unit 9

1 **Which of these sentences are correct (C) and incorrect (I)?**

1 We must to finish this by the end of the day. ___
2 You don't have to bring your computer. ___
3 They shouldn't eating so much cake. ___
4 He might be right about that. ___
5 Tonya ought join an athletics club. ___

6 Could you be explain this problem to me? ___
7 She needn't type out the whole report. ___
8 May I borrow your laptop? ___
9 Would you talking more quietly, please? ___
10 You should try to get some sleep. ___

How many did you get right? ☐

Grammar

Modals of permission

We can use *can* or *may* to ask for and give permission. *May* is formal and a little old-fashioned.
Can *I come to the technology fair with you?*
You ***can*** *work on the science project with us, if you like.*
May *I leave the class?*
You ***may*** *come into the examination hall now.*

We can use *be allowed to* to talk about permission (given by other people).
When I was younger, I ***was allowed*** *to play computer games at weekends, but I* ***wasn't allowed to*** *play them on school days.*

Modals of obligation

We use *must / mustn't* to talk about rules.
Lab coats ***must*** *be worn when doing science experiments.*
You ***must not*** *play around in the laboratory.*

We use *have to, need to* and *not be allowed to* to talk about rules (made by other people).
We ***have to / need to*** *wear lab coats for science experiments.*
They told us we ***weren't allowed to*** *play around in the laboratory.*

We use *not have to, not need to* or *need not* to say there is no rule (i.e. you can choose what to do).
You ***don't have / need to*** *wear safety goggles, but it's a good idea if you do.*
You ***needn't*** *bring a helmet – we have lots that you can borrow.*

Note

The nine main modal auxiliary verbs in English are: *can, could, may, might, shall, should, will, would* and *must*. Unlike most other verbs:

• they have no 's' for the *he / she / it* form: *he can*, not *he ~~cans~~*.
• they have no *-ing* form and no past participle.
• they are followed by an infinitive (without *to*): *I should ~~to~~ go*.
• we make negatives by adding *not* or *n't*: *can't, shouldn't, mightn't, won't*. There is no contraction for *may not*.
• we make questions by moving the modal verb before the subject: ***Should*** *I go?*

Note

Need to is usually used like a normal verb, but it can also be used as a modal verb, without *to*, in questions and negatives, although it sounds slightly old-fashioned.

Requests, recommendations, etc.

We can use *can*, *could*, *will* and *would* to make requests. *Could* and *would* are more polite.
***Can / Could / Will / Would** you charge my tablet, please?*

We use *must* to make strong recommendations and invitations.
*You **must** check out the latest photography app – it's brilliant!*
*You **must** come round for dinner with us soon.*

We use *should* to ask for and give advice and to state our expectations.
*You **should** get some rest – you look exhausted.* (= giving advice)
***Should** I get a newer phone?* (= asking for advice)
*I think you **should** ask before you use my tablet.* (= I expect you to do it)

We can use *ought to* instead of *should* to give advice, but it is not usually used in questions.
*You **ought to** revise before the test.*

We can use *be supposed to* to talk about other people's expectations.
*What **are we supposed to** do for homework?* (= What does our teacher expect us to do?)
*I **was supposed to** empty the dishwasher, but I forgot.*

We can use *could* to make weak suggestions.
*You **could** come along later, if you want.*

Modals of ability

We use *can / could / be able to* to talk about general ability in the present and past.
Be able to is a little more formal than *can* or *could*.
*Sally **can / is able to** count to ten in French and she's only five!*
*My sister **could / was able to** ride a bike when she was three.*

We can use *will be able to* to talk about future ability.
*I can't program a computer now, but hopefully I'**ll be able to** by the end of my course.*

To talk about ability or inability on a specific past occasion, we can use *couldn't* but not *could*.
Use *was able to* instead (or *managed to*).
*Unfortunately, I **couldn't / wasn't able to / didn't manage to** find my phone last night.*
*Luckily, I **was able to / managed to** find my phone last night.* (not: ~~I could find~~ …)

We can use *be capable of* to talk about the maximum limit of someone's / something's abilities.
*This drone **is capable of** flying for more than 30 minutes, apparently.*

Modals of logical deduction and probability

We use *must, may, might, could* and *can't* to make logical deductions about the present, i.e. to work something out based on evidence.

We use:
- *must* to say that we are sure that something is true.
*He **must be** happy, because he's studying his favourite subject.* (= I'm sure he is)
- *may, might* and *could* to say that we are not sure whether something is true or not.
*She **might** be the inventor – she looks familiar.* (= I'm not sure)
- *can't* to say that we are sure that something isn't true.
*He **can't** be a physicist; he doesn't like physics!* (= I'm sure he isn't)

We use *will / won't, should / shouldn't, may, might* and *could* to talk about the probability of future events.
The exam will / won't be very easy. (= I'm sure)
The exam should be very easy / shouldn't be too difficult. (= it's likely)
The exam may / might / could be easier than we think. (= it's possible)

Grammar exercises

2 **Choose the correct option to complete the sentences.**

1 Fortunately, *we can / were able to* reach the airport in time for our flight yesterday.
2 *Can I / Am I able to* use your phone charger, please?
3 Although I tried hard, I *could / couldn't* beat the club champion.
4 I'd like to *can / be able to* choose my own working hours.
5 *Can you / Could you* hear the teacher clearly this morning?
6 Both his sisters *can / were able to* play a reasonably good game of chess at the age of five.
7 We *can / could* see most of the city from our old house on the top of the hill.
8 Yes, you *can / could* borrow my games console at the weekend.
9 He *can't / wasn't able to* persuade his parents to let him go on holiday with his friends last summer.
10 Sally *couldn't / won't be able to* come to lunch tomorrow – she's working.

3 **Complete the sentences with *must / mustn't* or *don't / doesn't have to*.**

1 You _____ come with me if you don't want to.
2 Everyone _____ obey the law.
3 She _____ rush. She's got plenty of time.
4 Pete has a good broadband connection at home, so he _____ go to the office every day.
5 Children _____ touch electrical wires.
6 You _____ play your music quietly, or you will wake the baby.
7 I _____ go to bed early tonight – there's no school tomorrow!
8 Drivers _____ use their phones while driving.

4 **Write advice using *should / ought to* or *shouldn't*.**

1 I always hurt myself when I jump down the stairs.
   You shouldn't jump down the stairs! _____

2 Stephan doesn't practise the piano very much.
   _____

3 My head hurts and I have got a fever.
   _____

4 I can't close this suitcase because there are too many clothes in it.
   _____

5 Eating ice cream really hurts my teeth.
   _____

6 Pam really wants to buy a pet.
   _____

7 I get upset when I don't get 100% in a test.
   _____

8 I always write down my password so I don't forget it.
   _____

9

5 Rewrite the sentences using *may* or *might (not)*.

1 It is possible that these are my headphones, but I am not sure.
These _____.

2 Perhaps this is the app Kate mentioned.
This _____.

3 Perhaps she is browsing the internet.
She _____.

4 It is possible that he will not pass his exams.
He _____.

5 It is possible that Jack and Adam are flying the drone, but I am not sure.
Jack and Adam _____.

6 Perhaps Jonathan is not at the meeting.
Jonathan _____.

6 Rewrite the sentences using *can't* or *must*.

1 I am sure Susan isn't at work now. She left the office an hour ago.
Susan _____.

2 I am sure my brother is talking on the phone now. The line is busy.
My brother _____.

3 I am sure that Ben isn't studying in his room. I saw him in the garden.
Ben _____.

4 I am sure she is at the office now. I just spoke to her on the phone.
She _____.

5 I am sure my father isn't cooking again. I saw him cooking two hours ago.
My father _____.

6 I don't think my printer is broken. It was working ten minutes ago.
My printer _____.

7 Complete the second sentence so that it has a similar meaning to the first sentence, using the word given. Do not change the word given. You must use between two and five words.

1 It isn't necessary for you to upgrade your phone.
You _____ your phone. **HAVE**

2 I am sure Oscar is at the dentist's.
Oscar _____ the dentist's. **BE**

3 I am sure this isn't the place we are looking for.
This _____ we are looking for. **BE**

4 It is possible that we will win the game.
We _____ the game. **MIGHT**

5 I advise you to save your work regularly.
You _____ regularly. **OUGHT**

6 Molly managed to finish her report in one day.
Molly _____ her report in one day. **WAS**

7 It isn't necessary for you to buy a present for me.
You don't _____ a present. **NEED**

Vocabulary

Phrasal verbs

8 Match the phrasal verbs (1–8) with their meanings (a–h).

1	back up	☐	**a**	turn on a computer, light, etc.
2	break down	☐	**b**	make a spare copy of something on a computer
3	come up	☐	**c**	illegally enter another computer system
4	hack into	☐	**d**	talk more loudly
5	plug in	☐	**e**	appear on a screen
6	shut down	☐	**f**	turn off a computer
7	speak up	☐	**g**	suddenly stop working
8	switch on	☐	**h**	connect a machine to an electricity supply

9 Complete the sentences with the correct form of the phrasal verbs from Exercise 8.

1 Martin was arrested for _____ a company's computer system.

2 My laptop _____ last week and I can't afford to get it repaired.

3 It's too dark in here. Can you _____ the light, please?

4 How many results _____ when you searched for information?

5 I felt silly when I realised that the computer wasn't broken – it was simply not _____ .

6 You'll need to _____ because we can't hear you very well.

7 It was past midnight when I finally _____ my computer and went to bed.

8 Always _____ your work, because you might lose it forever if you don't.

Prepositions

10 Complete the sentences with these words. Use each word at least once.

at	for	in	on

1 We've arranged _____ someone to fix your car on Tuesday morning.

2 You shouldn't stare _____ a screen for longer than 20 minutes.

3 Too much screen time can result _____ eye problems.

4 I spoke to her _____ the phone last night.

5 If you write down your password, it's _____ risk of being discovered.

6 Dropping your phone in water is very bad _____ it!

Collocations and expressions

11 Complete the sentences with these words.

answering	cash	sewing	time	vending	washing

1 I am wearing the same clothes again because our _____ machine is broken.

2 If I had a _____ machine, I'd go back to the age of the dinosaurs.

3 Is there a _____ machine near here? I need a drink.

4 Fewer people are using _____ machines because they can pay with cards or phones.

5 Have you got a _____ machine? My jeans need to be repaired.

6 I hate talking to _____ machines. I usually just hang up without saying anything.

9

Words easily confused

12 Complete the sentences with the correct form of these words. Use each word at least once.

1 **bring carry fetch take**

   a I think I'll _____ the children to the Science Museum tomorrow.
   b We ordered tea and you've _____ us coffee.
   c Could someone help me _____ this TV – it's really heavy!
   d Please could you _____ that cable for me?

2 **avoid ban block forbid prevent**

   a This device _____ the engine from overheating.
   b How can I _____ speaking to her when we work in the same office?
   c He was _____ from the video call for shouting.
   d Taking photographs in this area is strictly _____ .
   e I didn't trust the sender of the message, so I _____ the number.

3 **affect cause happen lead**

   a What _____ to your car?
   b Drones can _____ accidents if they fly too close to planes.
   c The floods _____ several houses close to the river.
   d Several different factors _____ to the development of the internet.

4 **expand extend increase rise**

   a Many technology companies have _____ their profits.
   b Silicon Valley _____ along much of the Santa Clara Valley in California.
   c They're thinking of _____ their business.
   d If the temperature _____ any higher, turn on the air conditioning.
   e Gases _____ when heated.

Word formation mixed

13 Use the word in capitals to form a word that fits in the gap.

1 This motorbike has a very _____ engine.   **POWER**
2 The boy who saved me won a medal for _____ .   **BRAVE**
3 I use a _____ printer, so I don't need a cable to connect it to my laptop. **WIRE**
4 Were you able to open the _____ I sent you?   **ATTACH**
5 The _____ is planning to increase taxes again.   **GOVERN**
6 The two companies formed a _____ and became very successful.   **PARTNER**
7 I'm so _____ – I have never won anything in my life.   **LUCK**
8 That was an _____ thing to do!   **AMAZE**

Sentence transformation

14 Complete the second sentence so that it has a similar meaning to the first sentence, using the word given. Do not change the word given. You must use between two and five words.

1 I'm sure that Simon isn't 19 years old.

BE

Simon _____ 19 years old.

2 I advise you to go and see this film.

OUGHT

You _____ and see this film.

3 It wasn't necessary for them to prepare a meal for us.

HAVE

They _____ prepare a meal for us.

4 You should turn off your computer, to save energy.

SHUT

You should _____ your computer, to save energy.

5 I can go to work on my bike if my car stops working.

BREAKS

If my car _____ , I can go to work on my bike.

6 Always make a copy of your files.

BACK

Always _____ your files.

7 Heavy rain can sometimes cause floods in the streets near the river.

RESULT

Heavy rain can _____ floods in the streets near the river.

8 Someone is coming to replace my printer today. I've made a plan.

ARRANGED

I've _____ to come and replace my printer today.

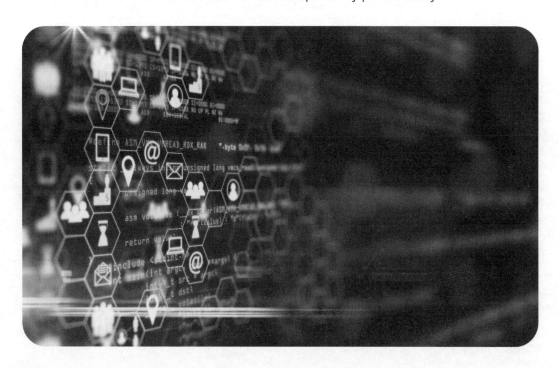

Unit 10

Awareness

1 **Which of these sentences are correct (C) and incorrect (I)?**

1 Tom might taken your coat by mistake. ___
2 You should have been practised more. ___
3 I could have been a great footballer. ___
4 He can't have driving home last night – he doesn't have a car. ___
5 That must have been a very exciting race. ___

6 I would lent it to you if you had asked. ___
7 We needn't have hurried because the show started late. ___
8 Sorry, should I asked permission first? ___
9 Would you have gone if you had been invited? ___
10 He shouldn't have been said that to her. ___

How many did you get right? ☐

Grammar

Perfect modals

We can use a modal auxiliary verb + *have* + past participle to talk about the past.

- We can use *must have, may have, might have, could have* and *can't have* to make logical deductions about the past.
Landing on the moon **must have been** *very exciting.* (= I'm sure it was)
Maria **may / might / could have picked up** *your headphones, but I'm not sure.*
They **can't have driven** *here – they haven't got a car.* (= I'm sure they didn't)

- We can use *would have, could have, might have* and *should have* or *ought to have* to imagine the unreal past.
I **would have lent** *you my phone charger, but you didn't ask me.*
Tom **could have been** *an engineer, but he decided to become an artist instead.*
You **should / ought to have taken** *your laptop back to the shop.* (= Why didn't you?)

- We use *needn't have* to say someone did something although it wasn't necessary. This is slightly different from the meaning of *didn't need to*.
I **needn't have printed** *the document – they had extra copies.* (= I did it, but it wasn't necessary)
I **didn't need to print** *the document – they said they had copies for everyone.* (= it wasn't necessary)

Grammar exercises

2 Write the words in order.

1 might / arrived / She / not / yet / have

_____

2 out / gone / have / My parents / may

_____

3 wanted / to come / Simon / not / have / might

_____

4 listening / might / been / have / I / to music

_____

5 well / Daniel / last night / been / not / might / feeling / have

_____

6 your / may / You / broken / finger / have

_____

3 Complete the sentences with *can't have* or *must have* and the correct form of the verbs.

1 **A:** Did they go to the cinema yesterday?
   B: They _____ (go) because there was no one at home when I called.

2 Kate is exhausted. She _____ (work) hard in the garden today.

3 Susan's telephone wasn't working yesterday. She _____ (phone) you.

4 She hadn't seen him before, so she _____ (recognise) him.

5 I called her twice, but she didn't answer the phone. She _____ (be) asleep.

6 **A:** John translated the email for me.
   B: John doesn't speak French, so he _____ (translate) it.

7 Emma has been at home all day. You _____ (see) her at the restaurant.

8 She asked me for money again. She _____ (spend) all the money I gave her.

4 Rewrite the sentences using *should have / shouldn't have*.

1 Tom was supposed to be sleeping.
   Tom _____ .

2 Julia was supposed to bring all the documents.
   Julia _____ .

3 My brother tried to fix his phone, but he made it worse.
   My brother _____ .

4 She didn't arrive on time for the rehearsal.
   She _____ .

5 Ben lied to his parents.
   Ben _____ .

6 My sister didn't mention the accident.
   My sister _____ .

10

5 Rewrite the sentences using *needn't have* or *didn't need to*.

1 It was unnecessary for you to bring all this food. You're very kind.

You _____ .

2 It wasn't necessary for me to get up early this morning; that's why I slept until late.

I _____ .

3 I didn't go shopping today. I went yesterday.

I _____ .

4 She watered the flowers this morning, but it rained later.

She _____ .

5 We didn't cook today. We had booked a restaurant.

We _____ .

6 I studied for the test, but it was incredibly easy.

I _____ .

6 Complete the second sentence so that it has a similar meaning to the first sentence, using the word given. Do not change the word given. You must use between two and five words.

1 Perhaps your son took your car.

Your son _____ your car. **HAVE**

2 I'm sure that you didn't see Mark in the city centre.

You _____ Mark in the city centre. **CAN'T**

3 I am sure someone has fixed this computer. It's much faster now.

Someone _____ this computer. **MUST**

4 Thank you very much for the present. It wasn't necessary.

You _____ a present. **BROUGHT**

5 You didn't ask your parents first.

You _____ first. **ASKED**

6 It was too big, so I didn't buy it.

I _____ if it had been smaller. **BOUGHT**

Vocabulary

Phrasal verbs

7 Match the phrasal verbs (1–8) with their meanings (a–h).

1 be taken in ☐   a find

2 get hold of ☐   b pay close attention to something to avoid anything bad happening

3 key in ☐   c join a computer network

4 log in ☐   d make the volume or heat lower

5 log out ☐   e be fooled or cheated by someone

6 turn down ☐   f make the volume or heat higher

7 turn up ☐   g type information into a computer or other machine

8 watch out for ☐   h disconnect from a computer network

8 Complete the sentences with the correct form of the phrasal verbs from Exercise 7.

1 I can't _____ to this account without a password.

2 Do you know where I can _____ some good speakers?

3 Can you _____ your music, please? I'm trying to work.

4 What problems should I _____ when I'm setting up a video call?

5 Don't _____ by emails asking for your bank details.

6 _____ the heating. It's freezing in here!

7 Always remember to _____ from your email account when you are using a public computer.

8 Could you _____ this data for me, please?

Prepositions

9 Complete the sentences with these words. Use each word at least once.

1 We've been experimenting *with / within / without* different designs for the app.

2 Our service engineer will call you *with / within / without* the next few days.

3 Please respond to this message *with / within / without* delay.

4 We managed to keep our spending on the project *with / within / without* budget.

5 The classrooms are equipped *with / within / without* tablets and a high-speed broadband connection.

6 How long do you think you could do *with / within / without* your phone?

Collocations and expressions

10 Complete the sentences with these words.

| attention   business   consideration   control   convenience   difference |

1 When you mark my exam, please take into _____ the fact that I was ill.

2 I have left my essay on your desk for you to read at your _____ .

3 It makes no _____ what I do – the screen is blank.

4 I'm sorry, but what happens from now on is beyond my _____ .

5 It's none of your _____ how much money I earn!

6 Try to catch the waiter's _____ – I want to ask for the bill.

Words easily confused

11 Complete the sentences with the correct form of these words. Use each word at least once.

1 arrive   get   reach

  a After an hour's walk, we _____ to the Science Museum.

  b She _____ at the technology fair in an electric car.

  c The plane is due to _____ the airport in 20 minutes.

2 angle   corner   edge   margin

  a Leave the bag in the _____ , next to the desk.

  b Let's look at the problem from a different _____ .

  c Don't write in the _____ because that's where the teacher makes her comments.

  d They stood at the water's _____ and gazed at the sunset.

3 certainly   likely   probably

  a Don't worry. There's _____ a simple reason why they're late.

  b It's _____ that Smith will win the race. She's the current champion.

  c I'm _____ not going to lend him my headset again! He broke it.

10

Word formation   mixed

12 Use the word in capitals to form a word that fits in the gap.

1 All of the _____ in the computer game were professional actors.   PERFORM
2 That's the _____ camera I have ever seen.   TINY
3 We see our cousins _____ every week on a video call.   VIRTUAL
4 I _____ spilled coffee all over my keyboard.   ACCIDENT
5 I _____ believe that the wheel is the greatest invention.   TRUE
6 Virtual _____ is used in education, medicine and sport, as well as gaming.   REAL
7 Thank you. Your _____ is really appreciated.   KIND
8 He was lucky to be _____ after an accident like that!   LIVE

Sentence transformation

13 Complete the second sentence so that it has a similar meaning to the first sentence, using the word given. Do not change the word given. You must use between two and five words.

1 It was a bad idea to spend so long browsing the internet.
   SPENT
   You _____ so long browsing the internet.

2 I didn't know about the exhibition, so I didn't go.
   WOULD
   I _____ the exhibition if I had known about it.

3 I am certain she was sleeping when I phoned her.
   BEEN
   She _____ when I phoned her.

4 Many people were fooled by a text which asked for their bank details.
   TAKEN
   Many people were _____ a text which asked for their bank details.

5 You should install anti-virus software as soon as possible.
   WITHOUT
   Install anti-virus software _____ .

6 You won't get those emails back, no matter what you do.
   DIFFERENCE
   It _____ what you do, you won't get those emails back.

7 I was trying to make her notice me, so that I could ask her for help.
   CATCH
   I was trying _____ , so that I could ask her for help.

8 You have no right to know my password, so don't ask me for it.
   NONE
   My password _____ , so don't ask me for it.

Unit 11

1 Which of these sentences are correct (C) and incorrect (I)?

1 Have you finished tidy your room? ___
2 Your bungalow will be cleaned daily. ___
3 I'm pleased to hear that you have recovered. ___
4 She persuaded him going on the rollercoaster. ___
5 It's not worth to worry about it. ___

6 We weren't allowed to use mobile phones. ___
7 The teacher made me write the essay again. ___
8 I wasn't expecting meet anyone I knew. ___
9 Steve had difficulty understanding the instructions. ___
10 Do you remember visiting this place before? ___

How many did you get right? ☐

Grammar

-ing form

We can use the -ing form:

- as the subject of a sentence or clause.
Running is my favourite type of exercise.
Are you sure that swimming straight after lunch is a good idea?

- after prepositions.
I'm so excited about coming to visit you.

- after the verb *go* when we talk about activities.
Emma goes skiing every winter.

We also use the -ing form after certain verbs and phrases:
admit, avoid, be used to, can't help, can't stand, deny, dislike, (don't) mind, enjoy, fancy, (don't) feel like, finish, forgive, hate, have difficulty, imagine, involve, it's no good, it's no use, it's (not) worth, keep, like, love, miss, practise, prefer, prevent, regret, risk, spend time.
I don't feel like cooking tonight.
It's worth paying a little bit more for a better bike.

to + infinitive

We use *to* + infinitive:

- to explain purpose.
We went into town to buy tickets for the concert.

- after adjectives such as *easy, difficult, afraid, scared, happy, glad, pleased, sad,* etc.
I find it difficult to do exercise first thing in the morning.

- after *too* + adjective or adjective + *enough*.
It was too wet to play tennis outside.
It wasn't cold enough to snow.

We also use *to* + infinitive after certain verbs and phrases:
afford, agree, appear, arrange, begin, choose, decide, expect, fail, forget, hope, learn, manage, mean, need, offer, plan, prepare, pretend, promise, refuse, seem, start, want, would like.
Anna and I agreed to run the race together.
Would you like to come to the cinema with us?

Infinitive (without *to*)

We use the infinitive (without *to*) after:

- modal verbs.

They **could win** the tournament.

- *had better* to give advice.

We **had better run** or we'll miss the train.

- *would rather* to talk about preference. We often use the word *than*.

I **would rather play** basketball **than** volleyball.

> **Note**
>
> We use *let* + object + infinitive when we want to say that we give permission for someone to do something, and it is only used in the active voice. In the passive we can use the verb *be allowed to*.
> Her parents **let her stay out** later at weekends.
> She **is allowed to stay out** later at weekends.

> **Note**
>
> We use *make* + object + infinitive when we want to say that we force a person to do something in the active voice. However, in the passive *make* is followed by *to* + infinitive.
> The coach **made us practise** hitting the ball at the net.
> We **were made to practise** hitting the ball at the net (by the coach).

> **Note**
>
> After the verb *help*, we can use either *to* + infinitive or the infinitive (without *to*). Both forms mean exactly the same.
> Can you **help me (to) learn** to juggle?

-ing form or *to* + infinitive?

Some verbs can be followed by an *-ing* form or *to* + infinitive with no change in meaning. Some common ones are *begin, bother, continue, hate, like, love* and *start*.
They've **started doing / to do** yoga on Tuesday evenings.
Sam has **continued playing / to play** hockey after leaving school.
I **hated doing / to do** jigsaw puzzles when I was a child.

There are other verbs that can be followed by an *-ing* form or *to* + infinitive, but the meaning changes. Some common ones are *forget, go on, mean, regret, remember, stop* and *try*.
I'll never **forget scoring** the winning goal in the final. (I'll always remember that it happened.)
I **forgot to bring** my trainers. (I didn't remember to bring my trainers, so I don't have them with me.)

We **went on running** through the rain. (We continued to run.)
She **went on to run** her fastest time ever. (She had been running, then after the point the speaker is referring to, she ran her fastest time ever.)

Being in the swimming team **means training** before school. (That's what it involves.)
I **meant to bring** my goggles, but I forgot. (I planned / intended to bring them.)

I **regret not going** to the trials for the basketball team. (I didn't go to the trials, but now I wish I had.)
We **regret to inform** you that the match has been cancelled. (We're sorry that we have to tell you this.)

My dad **remembers seeing** Usain Bolt in the Olympics. (He saw Usain Bolt and remembers seeing him.)
I **remembered to take** my helmet when I cycled to school. (I remembered first and then I took my helmet.)

We **stopped playing** because we were thirsty. (We didn't continue playing.)
We **stopped to have** a drink. (We stopped doing something so we could have a drink.)

Try calling the box office about the tickets. (See if you can call the box office about the tickets.)
I'll **try to book** tickets this afternoon. (I'll make an effort to book tickets this afternoon.)

Grammar exercises

2 **Choose the correct option to complete the sentences.**

1 It's no use *talking* / *to talk* to Adam – he won't listen to you.
2 You were so *lucky get* / *to have got* tickets for the cup final.
3 It was so kind of you *to take* / *taking* me to the theatre.
4 We should *learn* / *to learn* some Spanish before our trip.
5 My sister denied *taking* / *to take* my headphones without asking.
6 Sam couldn't afford *going* / *to go* on holiday this year.
7 We had better *to hurry* / *hurry*, or else we will miss the train.
8 Cara avoided *driving* / *to drive* in the rush hour when she lived in Paris.
9 My parents don't let me *staying up* / *stay up* late during the week.
10 Liam reminded me *entering* / *to enter* the race.

3 **Complete the sentences with the *-ing* or infinitive form (with or without *to*) of the verbs.**

1 Do you feel like _____ (go) out or would you rather _____ (stay) in tonight?
2 Did they manage _____ (carry) the new canoe to the river?
3 I always enjoy _____ (eat) out with friends.
4 I'd like _____ (eat) in a Chinese restaurant this weekend.
5 Oh no. I forgot _____ (lock) the door! I'd better _____ (go) back and _____ (do) it now.
6 After _____ (spend) two weeks away, she looked forward to _____ (see) us all.
7 He pretended _____ (be) sick in order to avoid _____ (go) to the circus.
8 I love amusement parks, but I'm scared of _____ (ride) on rollercoasters.

4 **Use the prompts to write sentences with the *-ing* or infinitive form (with or without *to*).**

1 I / not remember / get / a letter from you

_____

2 it / be / very kind / you / send / me / flowers / yesterday

_____

3 they / try / prevent / the spectators / from / run onto the pitch / last night

_____

4 they / accuse him of / sell fake tickets / last month / and finally / he admit / do it

_____

5 it / take / her / ages / get over / her illness / last year

_____

6 there / be / no point in / complain about / spend / so much money on the car

_____

7 he / be / the only student / pass / the exam

_____

8 my brother / spend / most of his free time / listen to music and / play computer games

_____

9 it / be / important / for me / relax / outdoors / and / be / close to nature

_____

10 it / be / impossible / for me / meet / you right now

_____

5 Rewrite the sentences using these verbs.

| accuse | admit | agree | apologise | deny | promise | refuse | suggest |

1 My sister said, 'No, I didn't take your sunglasses.'
   My sister _____ *denied taking* _____ my sunglasses.

2 Oscar said to me, 'No, I won't give you any money.'
   Oscar _____ me any money.

3 Dan said to Beth, 'I am so sorry I spoiled our holiday.'
   Dan _____ their holiday.

4 Martha said, 'Let's go sailing this weekend.'
   Martha _____ sailing that weekend.

5 Anna said to me, 'Yes, I'll help you with your homework.'
   Anna _____ me with my homework.

6 My brother said to me, 'You took my racket.'
   My brother _____ his racket.

7 I said, 'Yes, I borrowed your ball without asking .'
   I _____ my sister's ball without asking.

8 'Don't worry, Freddie. I'll take you to the park tomorrow,' said his father.
   Freddie's father _____ him to the park the next day.

6 Correct the sentences where necessary. Tick those which do not need correcting.

1 She couldn't cope with worked for so many hours a day.

   _____

2 Pam would rather to drink coffee than tea.

   _____

3 She admitted to steal the money from the safe.

   _____

4 Mr Anderson can't stand to be in the office all day.

   _____

5 They postponed going to see their grandparents.

   _____

6 I don't remember arranging a meeting for today.

   _____

7 Mike advised me working overtime to earn money for my holiday.

   _____

8 I don't enjoy to be in crowded places.

   _____

7 Complete the sentences about you.

1 I really can't afford _____ .

2 I spend my spare time _____ .

3 My parents don't let me _____ .

4 I am old enough _____ .

5 I really can't stand _____ .

6 I avoid _____ .

Vocabulary

Phrasal verbs

8 Match the phrasal verbs (1–8) with their meanings (a–h).

1 feel up to ☐   **a** meet with socially

2 get together ☐   **b** stop doing or trying to do something

3 give up ☐   **c** try to impress other people

4 knock over ☐   **d** show someone a place

5 run into ☐   **e** meet someone by chance

6 show around ☐   **f** arrive somewhere, usually unexpectedly

7 show off ☐   **g** be well or confident enough to do something

8 show up ☐   **h** hit someone / something and make them / it fall to the ground (including with a vehicle)

9 Complete the sentences with the correct form of the phrasal verbs from Exercise 8.

1 Let's stay at home tonight. I still don't _____ going out.

2 Every year the old school friends _____ for a meal.

3 The guide who _____ us _____ the museum was really friendly.

4 Ben is _____ because he wants to impress his teacher.

5 Zoe did gymnastics for six years, but she _____ last year.

6 Our cat has been _____ by a car twice, but he's still OK!

7 I _____ my old tennis coach at the supermarket yesterday.

8 We waited for half an hour for Simon to _____ , but he never did.

Prepositions

10 Choose the correct option to complete the sentences.

1 *On / In / At* second thoughts, I'd rather go to the tennis match tomorrow.

2 I'm *to / in / at* two minds about whether or not to go rock climbing this weekend.

3 If you're *on / in / at* a loose end, why not come round to my house and play computer games?

4 Athletics appeals *to / in / at* people in many different countries.

5 Shall we move *on / in / at* to the next point you wanted to discuss?

6 Has James told you his great idea? I think he's really *onto / into / out of* something.

Collocations and expressions

11 Complete the sentences with the correct form of *play*, *go* or *do*.

1 How often do you _____ climbing?

2 My aunt _____ yoga three times a week.

3 The only sport I enjoy _____ is volleyball.

4 Gary has been _____ karate for five years, and now he has a black belt.

5 Do you want to _____ bungee jumping with me next week?

6 I've _____ chess since I was eight years old, but I'm still not good at it.

11

Words easily confused

12 Complete the sentences with the correct form of these words. Use each word at least once.

1 `lead   medal   trophy   victory`

  a The captain of the winning team held up the winners' _____ .

  b With 400 metres of the race left, Jo was in the _____ by a few metres.

  c Three great goals gave the team a memorable _____ .

  d Very few gymnasts have won five Olympic gold _____ .

2 `logical   reasonable   sensible   sensitive`

  a She wears sunglasses because her eyes are _____ to light.

  b He's so _____ that he gets upset when you criticise him.

  c Julia was _____ enough to stop driving when she got too tired.

  d I tried to be _____ , but they refused to cooperate.

  e There's no _____ explanation for what happened.

3 `abandon   desert   disappear   mislay`

  a The weather was so bad that they had to _____ the search for the missing sailors.

  b Everyone _____ the beach when it started to rain.

  c As the fog came down, the mountains slowly _____ from view.

  d I seem to have _____ my goggles. Have you seen them?

4 `accurate   exact   precise`

  a My watch always tells the right time. It's very _____ .

  b The winners received a(n) _____ copy of the original trophy.

  c You said the film starts around eight o'clock. Can you be more _____ , please?

Word formation   mixed

13 Use the word in capitals to form a word that fits in the gap.

1 The team should be congratulated on such a _____ performance.   **MEMORY**

2 Before you go to university, you need to decide what subject you want to
_____ in.   **SPECIAL**

3 There is a _____ looking man hanging around outside the stadium.   **SUSPECT**

4 Tim decided not to play in the match because of the _____ in his shoulder.   **WEAK**

5 The crowd watched in _____ as the stunt rider performed his tricks.   **AMAZE**

6 This club has a large _____ , consisting of people of all ages.   **MEMBER**

7 Lucy is really _____ . She loves racing against other people.   **COMPETE**

8 I don't just _____ boxing, I hate it.   **LIKE**

Sentence transformation

14 Complete the second sentence so that it has a similar meaning to the first sentence, using the word given. Do not change the word given. You must use between two and five words.

1 'Let's go ice skating at the weekend,' said Julia.
   SUGGESTED
   Julia _____ at the weekend.

2 Driving without a licence is illegal.
   TO
   It's _____ a licence.

3 I'd buy these skis, but I don't have enough money.
   AFFORD
   I _____ these skis.

4 Jenny's mother thinks Jenny should join the basketball team.
   WANTS
   Jenny's mother _____ the basketball team.

5 The referee made the goalkeeper take the kick again.
   WAS
   The goalkeeper _____ the kick again.

6 I can't decide whether or not to go surfing tomorrow.
   MINDS
   I'm _____ whether or not to go surfing tomorrow.

7 I'm too tired to go for a run tonight.
   UP
   I don't _____ for a run tonight. I'm really tired.

8 I unexpectedly met Ian while I was watching the football match.
   RAN
   While I was watching the football match, _____ Ian.

Awareness

1 **Which of these sentences are correct (C) and incorrect (I)?**

1 I'd like to know when are you arriving. ___
2 You aren't very helpful, aren't you? ___
3 Wasn't that a great match? ___
4 Why you didn't tell me about this? ___
5 Could you to give me directions to the bank? ___

6 Let's go to the beach, shall we? ___
7 Don't talk so quickly, do you? ___
8 Doesn't she look lovely in that dress? ___
9 I'm very late, aren't I? ___
10 Do you know if Isabel is coming today? ___

How many did you get right? ☐

Grammar

Question tags

Question tags are short questions at the end of a sentence. They are formed with a modal or an auxiliary verb + a subject pronoun (*I, you, he, she, it, we* or *they*) or *there*.
We usually use an affirmative question tag after a negative sentence, and a negative question tag after an affirmative sentence.
*She has played all over the world, **hasn't she?***
*You can't solve this puzzle, **can you?***
*There were a lot of goals, **weren't there?***

When a sentence contains a verb in the present simple or the past simple (and doesn't use the verb *be*), *we use do / does, don't / doesn't* and *did / didn't* in the question tag.
*Ben loves windsurfing, **doesn't he?***
*They played really well, **didn't they?***

We use question tags when we want:
- someone to agree with what we are saying.
*That was a delicious meal, **wasn't it?***
- to make sure that what we are saying is right.
*We go to the same gym, **don't we?***

Remember

Some question tags are irregular. Notice the way these tags are formed.
I am** in the team, **aren't I?
Everyone is** happy, **aren't they?
Let's** go to the beach, **shall we?
Don't** drive so fast, **will you?
Wear** a helmet, **won't you?

Indirect questions

Indirect questions are used when we want to sound more formal, polite or distant. For indirect questions, we use the word order of a normal statement. We don't always need to use a full stop at the end.
***I'd like to know when** the tickets go on sale.*
***I wonder where** the football ground is.*

Questions for which the answer is *yes* or *no* use the word *if* or *whether*.
*Do you know **if** Marco is coming to the training session today?*
*Could you tell me **whether** I need to bring my own racket?*

Negative questions

Negative questions can be used:
- to show that we are surprised or doubtful.

Haven't you seen that film yet?
*Why **didn't** you want to play yesterday?*
- when we expect someone to agree with us.

*Wow! **Wasn't** that an amazing race?*
***Don't** the new team tracksuits look great?*

Note

When *not* is a separate word (for example in formal English), it comes after the subject.
*Did I **not** remind you about this?*

Grammar exercises

2 Choose the correct option to complete the sentences.

1 I'd *wonder / like* to know where you bought those trainers.
2 *Would / Could* you mind telling me where the exit is?
3 I don't *mind / suppose* you know how to get to the station from here.
4 Do you know *what / if* the other team has arrived yet?
5 I *suppose / wonder* if she would like to come to the art gallery.
6 *Do / Could* you tell me whether it's going to rain today?
7 I *could / would* like to ask you why the tickets are so expensive.

3 Complete the indirect questions.

1 Where is the changing room?
   Could you tell me _____ ?

2 How much does this cost?
   I wonder if you know _____ .

3 When do the tickets go on sale?
   I'm not sure if you know _____ .

4 Is that Wembley Stadium over there?
   Do you know _____ ?

5 Did the children enjoy the show?
   I'd like to ask you _____ .

6 What's the time?
   Would you mind _____ ?

4 Match the sentences (1–8) with the question tags (a–h).

1 You went to the practice on Monday,   a won't they?
2 There aren't any goggles by the pool,   b does it?
3 Let's turn off the television,   c aren't I?
4 They never win away from home,   d has she?
5 They'll be here soon,   e didn't you?
6 She's never beaten you at tennis,   f shall we?
7 It doesn't hurt,   g are there?
8 I am right,   h do they?

5 **Complete the questions with question tags.**

1 I'd better leave now, _____ ?

2 Patrick can't drive, _____ ?

3 He broke the world record last year, _____ ?

4 Help me with this assignment, _____ ?

5 Let's go swimming, _____ ?

6 Those are your boots, _____ ?

6 **Complete the negative questions.**

1 _____ the weather been terrible recently?

2 Why _____ Martha home until after midnight?

3 _____ it be great if Mum and Dad bought an electric car?

4 _____ you heard the news about the Olympics?

5 _____ they happy to have Sports Day at school yesterday?

6 _____ it a lovely day?

7 **Complete the sentences with one word in each gap.**

1 Do you know _____ Simon is at home?

2 They don't enjoy losing, _____ they?

3 _____ didn't they phone a taxi?

4 I'd _____ to know where you got those tickets.

5 Let's go to the park, _____ we?

6 Everyone loves chocolate, don't _____ ?

Vocabulary

Phrasal verbs

8 **Match the phrasal verbs (1–8) with their meanings (a–h).**

1	believe in	☐	**a** get out of bed later than usual
2	burst out	☐	**b** move at the same speed as someone / something
3	cut down on	☐	**c** become successful or popular very quickly
4	keep up with	☐	**d** reject an invitation
5	sleep in	☐	**e** begin doing something suddenly
6	stand back	☐	**f** move a short distance from something
7	take off	☐	**g** be sure that something is right
8	turn down	☐	**h** reduce the number or amount of something

9 **Complete the sentences with the correct form of the phrasal verbs from Exercise 8.**

1 The doctor advised my uncle to _____ the amount of sugar he eats.

2 Finn _____ his place at a university in London because he wanted to live near the sea.

3 I used to go running with Sarah, but she was so fast that I couldn't _____ her.

4 Sorry I'm late. I _____ this morning because my alarm didn't go off!

5 When Ellen saw the funny photo of herself, she _____ laughing.

6 When did your tennis career really start to _____ ?

7 Steve _____ always being honest with people, even if they might be offended.

8 You should _____ from the edge of the cycle track or you might get hit.

Prepositions

10 **Choose the correct option to complete the sentences.**

1 Why don't you want to come to the beach? What's wrong *for / of / with* you?

2 We can't afford another car, so this one will just have to do *for / of / with* the moment.

3 Is this just a rehearsal or is it *for / of / with* real?

4 Gymnastics requires a combination *for / of / with* strength and flexibility.

5 I am writing *for / of / with* reference to our recent stay at your hotel in Monaco.

6 Tom's new bike is just *for / of / with* mountain biking – not cycling to work.

Collocations and expressions

11 **Complete the sentences with these words.**

come	hold	know	make	put	take

1 I'm afraid I don't _____ the first thing about rugby.

2 It's fun playing tennis with my friends because we don't _____ ourselves too seriously.

3 Don't _____ your life at risk when you're climbing. Wear a helmet.

4 They are getting better, but they've never _____ close to winning a tournament.

5 Practising for a few minutes every day will really _____ a difference.

6 The club he played for as a boy will always _____ an important place in his heart.

Words easily confused

12 **Complete the sentences with the correct form of these words. Use each word at least once.**

1 | notice | observe | see | watch |
|---|---|---|---|

   a The zoologist spent days _____ the behaviour of the lions.

   b Can you _____ the top of the mountain?

   c It's such a small stain that no one will _____ it.

   d Would you rather _____ television or go out?

2 | coast | port | resort | seaside | shore |
|---|---|---|---|---|

   a A day at the _____ would be good fun.

   b Cannes is a popular tourist _____ .

   c We had a wonderful holiday sailing on the west _____ of Ireland.

   d Our boat sank, but we were able to swim to the _____ .

   e Large cruise ships are too big for this small _____ .

3 | commentator | correspondent | editor | reporter |
|---|---|---|---|

   a A(n) _____ decides which articles are included in a newspaper.

   b He's worked as an arts _____ for the last ten years.

   c At the start of the football match, the _____ predicted a win for Brazil.

   d The _____ asked the manager some tricky questions at the press conference.

4 | qualification | skill | talent |
|---|---|---|

   a She has all the necessary _____ for the job.

   b On paper, the candidate had plenty of _____ , but very little experience.

   c Nowadays, _____ scouts try to sign children at a very young age.

12

13 Use the word in capitals to form a word that fits in the gap.

1 My father is a professional _____ who works for the government.   **ECONOMY**

2 Tanya stared at the chess board _____ and considered her next move.   **THOUGHT**

3 If you get a reputation for _____ , nobody will want you on their team.   **HONEST**

4 The competitors weren't distracted by the _____ of so many spectators.   **PRESENT**

5 My _____ for a holiday destination is probably different from yours.   **PREFER**

6 We haven't got an _____ supply of money, you know.   **END**

7 You shouldn't argue with the referee, even if you _____ with her decision.   **AGREE**

8 I can't do this puzzle – it's _____ !   **POSSIBLE**

Sentence transformation

14 Complete the second sentence so that it has a similar meaning to the first sentence, using the word given. Do not change the word given. You must use between two and five words.

1 Are there any tickets left?

WHETHER

Could you _____ any tickets left?

2 When does the train arrive in Coventry?

WHEN

I'd like to know _____ in Coventry.

3 I'm sure you'll agree that the concert was fantastic.

WASN'T

The concert _____ ?

4 Step away from the doors, or you might fall out.

STAND

You might fall out if you _____ from the doors.

5 She was invited to the party, but she decided not to go.

DOWN

She _____ the invitation to the party.

6 You should reduce the amount of chocolate you eat.

CUT

You _____ the amount of chocolate you eat.

7 Let's sit down and rest here for now.

MOMENT

For _____ , let's sit down and rest here.

8 I'm writing about your job advert.

REFERENCE

I'm writing _____ your job advert.

B2 Practice: First

Part 1

For questions 1–8, read the text below and decide which answer (A, B, C or D) best fits each gap. There is an example at the beginning (0).

A new breed of superstar

Nowadays, many people become household names through professions that were once **(0)** ___ of as simply respectable, rather than glamorous. Take lawyers, for example. Getting a job with a top law firm may not only ensure financial security due to the astronomical **(1)** ___ lawyers can command, but it may also bring the same superstar **(2)** ___ as that of a Hollywood actor – or lead to a career in politics. There are few people who do not **(3)** ___ the names of Bill and Hillary Clinton or Barak Obama.

But a person must be cut out to be a lawyer in order to be successful. Firstly, a persuasive character is essential. Secondly, the **(4)** ___ to judge character is vital, since a witness's **(5)** ___ to a question may be more significant than the answer given. **(6)** ___ , leadership qualities are fundamental. Top lawyers do not have the time to **(7)** ___ all the research necessary in a case by themselves. As a **(8)** ___ , they have to set an example for those under their command, so that they can count on the team to work conscientiously.

0	**A** looked	**B** regarded	**C** considered	**(D)** thought
1	**A** tips	**B** fares	**C** rewards	**D** fees
2	**A** level	**B** fame	**C** status	**D** stance
3	**A** recognise	**B** remind	**C** memorise	**D** retain
4	**A** certainty	**B** capability	**C** will	**D** ability
5	**A** look	**B** reaction	**C** action	**D** response
6	**A** Eventually	**B** Finally	**C** Ultimately	**D** Conclusively
7	**A** do	**B** take	**C** make	**D** carry
8	**A** end	**B** score	**C** result	**D** sum

Part 2

For questions 9–16, read the text below and think of the word which best fits each gap. Use only one word in each gap. There is an example at the beginning (0).

Robert Burns

Robert Burns, Scotland's greatest poet, **(0)** ____was____ born in 1759. From an early age he had to help his father on his farm, as **(9)** _____ as attend school lessons. When he was 22, he moved to Irvine, where he began to learn about making cloth. Shortly after **(10)** _____ arrival, the factory in which he was training was destroyed by fire, so he started a farm with his younger brother Gilbert.

While he was living on the farm, Robert concentrated **(11)** _____ writing poems. He fell for a local girl, Jean Armour, and wanted to marry her, but her father **(12)** _____ not allow him to do so. This took Robert **(13)** _____ surprise, and since he could not **(14)** _____ used to the idea of being unable to marry her, he decided to leave the country. Just as he was about to leave, he was advised to publish some of the poems he **(15)** _____ written. He received a large sum of money for the poetry and was then **(16)** _____ to get married to Jean.

Part 3

For questions 17–24, read the text below. Use the word given in capitals at the end of some of the lines to form a word that fits in the gap in the same line. There is an example at the beginning (0).

Extreme sports

In the past few years, extreme sports have **(0)** _____greatly_____ increased in popularity, **GREAT**

particularly among young, well-paid professionals. But why do people take up such apparently

(17) _____ activities? What is the attraction of doing things like bungee jumping, **DANGER**

hang-gliding, or jumping off a cliff with a parachute? Extreme sports lovers say they get no **SATISFY**

(18) _____ from traditional sports or even **(19)** _____ . They **ATHLETE**

claim that their boring daily routine does not **(20)** _____ them to live life to the **ABLE**

full. Only when putting their lives at risk do they feel truly alive.

Nowadays, there are extreme sports competitions in which those people courageous enough to

face the challenge of these **(21)** _____ new activities can win large cash prizes. **REVOLUTION**

This, in turn, has increased their popularity, and has resulted in the **(22)** _____ of **CREATE**

a whole new industry which specialises in making **(23)** _____ and clothing for **EQUIP**

extreme games. It has become a multi-million dollar business. Often the **(24)** _____ **DISCOVER**

that certain games have become commercial causes other people to come up with even more

extreme sports and the cycle is repeated.

Part 4

For questions 25–30, complete the second sentence so that it has a similar meaning to the first sentence, using the word given. Do not change the word given. You must use between two and five words, including the word given. Here is an example (0).

Example:

0 Jake couldn't fix the computer himself.

MANAGE

Jake _____ *didn't manage to* _____ fix the computer himself.

25 The house was completely empty.

FURNITURE

There _____ the house.

26 I'm sure they were asleep during the film.

MUST

They _____ during the film.

27 My dentist's advice was to reduce the amount of sugar I ate.

ADVISED

My _____ down on sugar.

28 When we got to Dover, the ferry wasn't there.

ALREADY

The ferry _____ the time we got to Dover.

29 Ingrid and Astrid have had many arguments in the past.

FALLEN

It's not the first time Ingrid _____ Astrid.

30 You need to be determined as well as skilful in order to be a professional athlete.

CALLS

Being a professional athlete _____ and determination.

B2 Practice: ECCE

Grammar

For questions 1–20, choose the word or phrase that best completes the sentence.

1 We might have been ___ about the start time.
  - A mistook
  - B mistaken
  - C mistake
  - D mistaking

2 Alex should never ___ bought that cheap car.
  - A have
  - B had
  - C been
  - D of

3 I'd like to ___ who stole my laptop.
  - A tell
  - B know
  - C believe
  - D suppose

4 Those ships are all from the same country, ___ ?
  - A aren't they
  - B aren't those
  - C they are
  - D those aren't

5 Why are you pretending ___ a bad leg?
  - A having
  - B to have
  - C have
  - D to having

6 ___ you ever tasted spinach?
  - A Didn't
  - B Aren't
  - C Haven't
  - D Weren't

7 Can you imagine ___ an Olympic medal?
  - A winning
  - B to win
  - C win
  - D to winning

8 Our car broke ___ on the way to the opera.
  - A up
  - B out
  - C in
  - D down

9 My dad made me ___ his car this morning.
  - A cleaning
  - B to clean
  - C clean
  - D to cleaning

10 It was very kind of you to help. You didn't ___ .
  - A should
  - B might
  - C have to
  - D may

11 Luckily, we ___ finish the match before it rained.
  - A were able to
  - B weren't able to
  - C had to
  - D wouldn't

12 They ___ have missed the train – I left them at the station with plenty of time to spare!
  - A must
  - B mustn't
  - C can't
  - D could

13 Let's have a game of tennis, ___ ?
  - A have we
  - B let we
  - C will we
  - D shall we

14 He ___ be a grandfather. He looks so young!
  - A mustn't
  - B needn't
  - C couldn't
  - D can't

15 When we were young, we ___ climb trees.
  - A used
  - B would
  - C may
  - D should

16 I prefer watching football ___ it.
  - A playing
  - B to play
  - C play
  - D to playing

17 You ___ have asked. You knew he would say 'no'.
  - A couldn't
  - B should
  - C needn't
  - D didn't

18 You really ___ to practise a bit more.
  - A should
  - B ought
  - C must
  - D could

19 Toby's a careless rider, ___ ?
  - A is he
  - B does he
  - C isn't he
  - D hasn't he

20 I think she'd rather ___ out than stay home.
  - A to go
  - B go
  - C going
  - D went

Vocabulary

For questions 21–40, choose the word or phrase that most appropriately completes the sentence.

21 I'm afraid what happens next is beyond my ___ .
A aim
B influence
C control
D ability

22 If you're at a loose ___ , we could go to the park.
A ending
B final
C finish
D end

23 Jo doesn't ___ up to going back to school yet.
A feel
B make
C look
D live

24 Simon has given ___ football to play more hockey.
A out
B on
C up
D over

25 When are you next ___ hiking in the mountains?
A coming
B going
C doing
D playing

26 It doesn't ___ any difference how much you offer to pay him.
A do
B make
C have
D hold

27 Can you ___ in to your Facebook account?
A log
B go
C key
D turn

28 There's a ___ machine selling snacks.
A cash
B washing
C vending
D sewing

29 Too much exercise can be bad ___ you.
A for
B of
C from
D at

30 Are we playing for ___ now?
A true
B honest
C real
D fact

31 On second ___ , let's just stay in and watch TV.
A beliefs
B thoughts
C thinks
D ideas

32 Why did he turn ___ the job?
A up
B off
C down
D around

33 What's wrong ___ the tablet? It isn't working.
A within
B with
C from
D for

34 We missed the flight because we slept ___ .
A in
B on
C under
D over

35 Don't forget to ___ some food with you.
A fetch
B carry
C hold
D bring

36 We're experimenting ___ a new IT system.
A with
B for
C from
D in

37 Let's all get ___ for a coffee and a chat.
A in
B around
C about
D together

38 Somebody has hacked ___ my computer and stolen my passwords.
A over
B on
C into
D off

39 Turn the music ___ . I can't hear it.
A down
B off
C out
D up

40 I'll give you a call ___ the next hour or so.
A within
B without
C among
D along

Awareness

1 Which of these sentences are correct (C) and incorrect (I)?

1 Our car was stole last week. ___
2 I'm being attacked by a gang of youths. ___
3 The suspect is been taken to the police station. ___
4 You'll be being given a new identity badge. ___
5 What will be done about the problems? ___

6 This project must be finished by next week. ___
7 He is believed that crime is falling. ___
8 This street hasn't been cleaned for weeks. ___
9 This area is being said to be the safest in the city. ___
10 You won't be told about our decision until later. ___

How many did you get right? ☐

Grammar

The passive

We use the passive when:

- the action is more important than who or what is responsible for it (the agent).

*The burglar **was arrested** yesterday evening.*

- we don't know the agent, or it is not important.

*Surveys **are used** to investigate people's preferences.*

- we want to draw particular attention to the agent by moving it to the end.

*The vandals **were caught** by a dog walker.*

> **Note**
>
> When it is important to mention the agent in a passive sentence, we use the word *by*. When we want to mention a tool or material, we use *with*.
> *The stolen goods **were found by** some children.*
> *The window **was broken with** a large rock.*
> *The house **is equipped with** a burglar alarm.*

The passive is formed with the verb **be** and a past participle. Notice how active verb forms change to passive forms. There is no passive form for the future continuous, present perfect continuous or past perfect continuous.

Tense	Active	Passive
present simple	take / takes	am / are / is taken
present continuous	am / are / is taking	am / are / is being taken
past simple	took	was / were taken
past continuous	was / were taking	was / were being taken
present perfect simple	have / has taken	have / has been taken
past perfect simple	had taken	had been taken
will	will take	will be taken

The object of the verb in the active sentence becomes the subject of the verb in the passive sentence. The verb *be* is used in the same tense of the main verb in the active sentence, together with the past participle of the main verb in the active sentence.

*They **were chasing** him. He **was being chased**.*
In this example we do not know who was chasing him and it is not very important, so we do not include this information in the passive sentence.

It's often possible to change a prepositional object in an active sentence into the subject of a passive sentence. The preposition remains in its original position after the verb, without an object.
*They didn't pay **for the magazines**.*
*The magazines weren't paid **for**.*

> **Note**
>
> After some verbs there are two objects, for example, *give*, *lend*, *send* and *show*. When we want to change an active sentence with two objects into the passive voice, one becomes the subject of the passive sentence and the other one remains an object. Which object we choose depends on what we want to emphasise. The structure is: subject [indirect object] + passive verb + direct object (+ by + agent).
> *She **was given the documents** (by her boss).*
> OR subject [direct object] + passive verb + indirect object (+ by + agent). When a direct object is followed by an indirect object, we have to use a preposition (*to*, *for*, etc.) in front of the indirect object.
> *The documents **were given to her** (by her boss).*

The passive: -ing form, infinitives and modal verbs

Tense	Active	Passive
-ing form	taking	being taken
Infinitive	take	be taken
to + infinitive	to take	to be taken
Modal	can take	can be taken

*The criminals tried to avoid **being seen**.*
*This report had better **be completed** by the end of today.*
*She agreed **to be transferred** to another police station.*
*Any unusual activity **must be reported** as soon as possible.*

We form the impersonal passive structure with: *it* + passive verb + *that* + clause.
Many people believe that poverty increases crime.
***It is believed that** poverty increases crime.*

We form the personal structure with noun + passive verb + *to* + infinitive.
People say that alarms deter burglars.
***Alarms are said to** deter burglars.*

> **Note**
>
> We often use verbs like *believe, consider, know, expect, say, suppose* and *think* in the passive. They can be used in an impersonal or a personal passive structure.

Grammar exercises

2 Choose the correct option to complete the sentences.

1 Fingerprints are *been / being* taken at the moment.
2 Two young men were *hurting / hurt* yesterday in an accident.
3 The detective is going to be *promoted / promote* next week.
4 He has never *be / been* suspected of theft before.
5 The jury will *be sat / have been sitting* for three weeks by the end of tomorrow.
6 Two football fans were *arrested / arresting* yesterday.
7 A window was *broke / broken* at school yesterday and I was *accusing / accused* of doing it.
8 The crime figures for the city are *publishing / published* every month.
9 Phones *don't / aren't* allowed in the courtroom.
10 A statement was *took / taken* immediately after the incident.

3 Write sentences in the passive.

1 They report the crime. The crime _____ .
2 They are reporting the crime. The crime _____ .
3 They reported the crime. The crime _____ .
4 They were reporting the crime. The crime _____ .
5 They have reported the crime. The crime _____ .
6 They had reported the crime. The crime _____ .
7 They will report the crime. The crime _____ .
8 They are going to report the crime. The crime _____ .
9 They will have reported the crime. The crime _____ .

13

4 Complete the sentences with the active or passive form of the verbs.

1 A message _____ (send) to me yesterday.

2 Sam _____ (not / invite) me to his party last Saturday.

3 The package _____ (deliver) to him by post.

4 He _____ (write) a report at the moment. He can't speak to you.

5 Your phone can't _____ (repair). You should _____ (get) a new one.

6 Your letter _____ (not / post) yet.

5 Write sentences in the passive.

1 You mustn't share your passwords with anyone.
Passwords _____.

2 He must deliver this parcel right away.
This _____.

3 He can't have broken the vase.
The _____.

4 We must bring identification to the interview.
Identification _____.

5 She has to make all the preparations for the trial.
All the preparations _____.

6 We don't have to clean the room now.
The room _____.

7 We should take the child to his parents' house.
The child _____.

8 He might have taken the book by mistake.
The book _____.

6 Rewrite the sentences.

1 They believe that the suspect lives in the area.
a It _____.
b The suspect _____.

2 They say that violent crime rates increase in hot weather.
a It _____.
b Violent crime rates _____.

3 They expect that he will get a fine for speeding.
a It _____.
b He _____.

4 People know that the inspector works very hard.
a It _____.
b The inspector _____.

5 People understand that politicians sometimes lie.
a It _____.
b Politicians _____.

6 They think that the burglars came in through the bathroom window.
a It _____.
b The burglars _____.

7 Complete the second sentence so that it has a similar meaning to the first sentence, using the word given. Do not change the word given. You must use between two and five words.

1 They told you to be here at ten.
You _____ at ten. **BE**

2 They are investigating the case at the moment.
The case _____ at the moment. **IS**

3 They have just fitted new locks.
New locks _____ fitted. **BEEN**

4 They might vandalise that old cinema.
That old cinema _____ . **VANDALISED**

5 Someone gave me some helpful advice.
I _____ some helpful advice. **WAS**

6 You had better pay that parking fine within 14 days.
That parking fine _____ within 14 days. **PAID**

7 We sell crime novels on the second floor.
Crime novels _____ on the second floor. **SOLD**

8 I hate it when my brother tricks me.
I can't _____ by my brother. **STAND**

Vocabulary

Phrasal verbs

8 Match the phrasal verbs (1–8) with their meanings (a–h).

1 burn down ☐   a not be punished for doing something wrong
2 do away with ☐   b kill or get rid of
3 do up ☐   c surrender to the police
4 get away with ☐   d rob
5 give yourself up ☐   e fix or decorate something, so that it looks good
6 give away ☐   f destroy something (usually a building) with fire
7 hold up ☐   g die
8 pass away ☐   h give something to someone for free

9 Complete the sentences with the correct form of the phrasal verbs from Exercise 8.

1 The criminals _____ the crime because the police never found them.
2 They are _____ free bottles of water in the park today.
3 Three men _____ the bank in the high street this afternoon, but they were soon arrested.
4 After they started the fire, the whole building _____ within minutes.
5 The kidnappers finally _____ , and are now in jail.
6 My grandfather _____ peacefully in his sleep at the age of 85.
7 Have you heard that they are _____ the old clubhouse, to make it look nice again?
8 The pupils at our school hope to _____ school uniform soon, because it is very unpopular.

13

Prepositions

10 Choose the correct option to complete the sentences.

1 You can't do that – it's *against / under / to* the law.

2 Barry is *against / under / of* suspicion of having taken part in a robbery.

3 Eventually, she confessed *against / under / to* stealing the phone.

4 Come with us, sir. You are *against / under / of* arrest.

5 The murderer was sentenced *against / under / to* a lifetime in prison.

6 After a long trial, the suspect was found guilty *against / under / of* the crime.

Collocations and expressions

11 Complete the sentences with the correct form of these words.

break   care   give   have   make   take

1 You have to _____ responsibility for your actions – you can't blame anyone else.

2 My friend recommended the new crime drama, so I'm going to _____ it a go.

3 I don't want to _____ a fool of myself by forgetting what to say.

4 I couldn't _____ less about losing the money, but the wallet was a gift from my aunt.

5 I don't want to get a new phone, but I _____ no choice.

6 He is one of the few people I know who didn't have to _____ the law to get rich!

Words easily confused

12 Complete the sentences with the correct form of these words. Use each word at least once.

1 accuse   commit   confess   suspect

   a Many people _____ Harry of stealing the phone, but they couldn't be sure.

   b After checking the speed camera, the police _____ Sue of dangerous driving.

   c Do you think it's ever OK to _____ a crime?

   d After several hours of questioning, she finally _____ to the crime.

2 glance   sight   view   vision

   a Just one _____ at the man was enough to prompt the doctor to call an ambulance.

   b The _____ from the helicopter was amazing.

   c Stay out of _____ until they've gone.

   d These glasses will improve your _____ .

   e The police waited quietly, hoping to catch _____ of the criminals.

3 inhabitant   neighbour   resident   tenant

   a They don't own the flat. They're _____ .

   b You can't park here. I'm afraid parking is only for _____ .

   c Our next-door _____ were burgled yesterday.

   d The _____ of this island have some very interesting customs.

4 court   jury   sentence   trial

   a During the _____ , several witnesses made false statements.

   b The _____ consisted of seven men and five women.

   c If we can't agree on a solution, the matter will have to be settled in _____ .

   d The blackmailer received a three-year prison _____ .

Word formation mixed

13 Use the word in capitals to form a word that fits in the gap.

1 Have you heard about the _____ at the local shop today? **ROB**

2 I have always suspected that Mark was a _____ . **CRIME**

3 The neighbours were worried after the second _____ in two weeks. **BURGLAR**

4 _____ is a problem for governments and citizens the world over. **TERROR**

5 Passengers were told to leave the airport after staff discovered a _____ package. **SUSPECT**

6 Offering money to a police officer is a serious _____ . **OFFEND**

7 You can't drive at that speed on this road – it's _____ . **LEGAL**

8 Do you think _____ is effective in preventing crime? **PUNISH**

Sentence transformation

14 Complete the second sentence so that it has a similar meaning to the first sentence, using the word given. Do not change the word given. You must use between two and five words.

1 They believe the event will be a huge success.

BELIEVED

It _____ will be a huge success.

2 Your dog can't have eaten your homework!

BEEN

Your homework _____ by your dog!

3 They say that area is dangerous after dark.

SAID

That area _____ dangerous after dark.

4 She hates it when people lie to her.

STAND

She _____ to.

5 You don't have to pay the bill straight away.

PAID

The bill doesn't _____ straight away.

6 It is time to get rid of this ridiculous law.

AWAY

It is time _____ this ridiculous law.

7 People suspect she's a hacker.

SUSPICION

She's _____ a hacker.

8 The shoplifters eventually admitted their crime and went with the police.

GAVE

The shoplifters eventually _____ to the police.

Awareness

1 Which of these sentences are correct (C) and incorrect (I)?

1 We have had smoke alarms installed in every room. ___

2 I'm used to have my nails done every month. ___

3 He got his wallet stolen on holiday. ___

4 We'll have our car serviced soon. ___

5 Did you get your photo taken by the police? ___

6 Have you have had your hair trimmed? ___

7 They were getting their bikes repaired when I saw them. ___

8 What time are you to having your hair cut? ___

9 She lost her passport, but got it replaced. ___

10 Did you use to get your mum to clean your shoes? ___

How many did you get right? ☐

Grammar

Causatives

We use the causative passive:

- to say that someone has arranged for someone else to do something for them.

Many people **have locks fitted** *to their garage doors.*

- to say that something unpleasant happened to someone.

We **had our flat broken into** *while we were on holiday.*

We form the causative with *have* + object + past participle. It can be used in a variety of tenses. When we want to mention the agent, we use the word *by*.

My grandmother **has had** *an alarm* **fitted**.

We **used to have** *our car* **serviced** *every year.*

You **will have** *your passport* **checked** *(by passport control).*

We use the causative active to say that someone asks or tells someone else to do something for them, when we want to emphasise the agent. We form the causative active with *get* + object + *to* + infinitive or *have* + object + infinitive (without *to*). It can be used in a variety of tenses. The version with *have* is much less common. We can only use it if the subject has the authority to tell other people to do things (e.g. he / she is the boss).

Can you **get someone to fix** *this?* (Can you ask / tell him / her to do it?)

I'll **have an officer take** *your fingerprints.* (I'll instruct him / her to do it.)

Note

For something that someone has arranged to have done, we can also use *get* + object + past participle. This structure is less formal. We don't usually use this to talk about unpleasant events.

I **got** *my glasses* **repaired** *at the optician's.*

Grammar exercises

2 Choose the correct option to complete the sentences.

1 Dad *had / has got* his car washed yesterday.

2 It's going to be a hot summer. We must *get / to have* air conditioning put in.

3 It's three years since we last had the bedroom walls *paint / painted* .

4 *I get / I'm getting* my computer fixed at the moment.

5 Terry is going to *have / get* her dad check her work before she hands it in.

6 The inspector is *having / to get* the whole house checked for fingerprints.

7 Sally *had / got* her arm broken in a climbing accident.

8 I'll *have / get* a plumber to have a look at our bathroom taps.

3 Complete the sentences with the causative form of the verbs.

1 We _____ last week. (our roof / repair)

2 She _____ yet. (not / her passport photo / take)

3 He _____ at the moment. (his ears / check)

4 They _____ when I called in this morning. (the alarm / replace)

5 Paul _____ once a year. (his carpets / clean)

6 We _____ once since we moved in. (the flat / redecorate)

7 I _____ by nine o'clock yesterday. (already / my eyes / test)

8 I have called a plumber. I _____ before you arrive. (the tap / fix)

4 Rewrite the sentences using the causative.

1 Someone stole my camera.

I _____ .

2 They are servicing my car.

I _____ .

3 Someone broke into my aunt's house.

My aunt _____ .

4 The hairdresser is going to cut my hair tomorrow.

I am _____ .

5 An electrician fixed the TV for Mary.

Mary _____ .

6 The dentist is filling one of my teeth.

I am _____ .

5 Write questions for the answers in bold. Use the causative.

1 _____ ?

I have my hair cut by **my brother**.

2 _____ ?

I'm going to get **Mr Walker** to service my car.

3 _____ ?

I had my room painted **last month**.

4 _____ ?

I need to get **my watch fixed**.

5 _____ ?

I get my little sister to clean **my room**.

6 _____ ?

I have my teeth checked **every six months**.

7 _____ ?

I've had my computer upgraded **because it was so slow**.

8 _____ ?

I'll be having my dress made **at Divine Designs**.

6 Complete the second sentence so that it has a similar meaning to the first sentence, using the word given. Do not change the word given. You must use between two and five words.

1 They have already published three books of mine.

I've _____ three books published by them.   **HAD**

2 We had our boiler fixed by a plumber.

We _____ our boiler.   **GOT**

3 Our floor needs polishing before the party.

We must _____ before the party.   **POLISHED**

4 Joe's mother washes his clothes.

Joe _____ his mother.   **GETS**

5 Is someone going to fix your teeth for you?

Are you _____ fixed?   **HAVE**

6 They will deliver Carol's new fridge tomorrow.

Carol will _____ tomorrow.   **DELIVERED**

Vocabulary

Phrasal verbs

7 Match the phrasal verbs (1–8) with their meanings (a–h).

1 go off	☐	**a**	put someone in prison
2 own up	☐	**b**	realise someone is trying to trick you
3 put away	☐	**c**	leave or escape suddenly
4 put down	☐	**d**	admit to doing something wrong
5 put off	☐	**e**	write someone's name on a document
6 run away	☐	**f**	make someone dislike something
7 see through	☐	**g**	make a sudden loud noise
8 see to	☐	**h**	deal with something that needs attention

8 Complete the sentences with the correct form of the phrasal verbs from Exercise 7.

1 He tried to trick me, but I _____ his plan.

2 The cat looked terrified when the alarm _____ .

3 I think Eva broke your computer, but she'll never _____ to it.

4 They caught the criminal and _____ him _____ for 25 years.

5 Shall I _____ your name for the neighbourhood watch scheme?

6 Don't worry about the broken window – I'll _____ it when I get home.

7 The vandals _____ when they heard the police sirens.

8 We were going to go to the park, but were _____ by the graffiti and vandalism.

Prepositions

9 Choose the correct option to complete the sentences.

1 Nobody likes being accused *of / from / in* a crime they didn't commit.
2 Police arrested the teenagers *of / for / in* vandalising the playground.
3 He picked up the jewellery and hid it *of / from / in* sight in his jacket.
4 I don't think she'll go to prison – I'm sure she is innocent *of / for / in* the crime.
5 After he was caught speeding through town, the man was banned *of / from / in* driving for six months.
6 The police were watching her, as they suspected her *of / for / in* committing several crimes.

Collocations and expressions

10 Complete the sentences with these words.

eye   justice   sentence   service   track   ways

1 Steve had to do community _____ when he got caught painting graffiti on the park walls.
2 If they ever catch the killer, he'll be given a life _____ .
3 The detective was so focused on the investigation that she lost _____ of time.
4 Sometimes, criminals can change their _____ and stop committing crimes.
5 Keep a(n) _____ on your bag – there are pickpockets in this part of town.
6 When the robbers were sent to prison, I felt that _____ had been done.

Words easily confused

11 Complete the sentences with the correct form of these words. Use each word at least once.

1 contain   form   hold   include   involve

   a My job _____ travelling abroad quite frequently.
   b The price _____ airport taxes and transfers.
   c Wood _____ only a small part of the structure of these houses.
   d Nobody knew exactly what the box _____ .
   e We need a suitcase that can _____ at least 15 kg.

2 inland   inner   interior   internal

   a We'd better get an _____ decorator to do the work.
   b His injuries are superficial and there's no _____ bleeding.
   c The village is about ten miles _____ , not on the coast.
   d There is a great deal of poverty in some _____ city areas.

3 carry out   celebrate   hold   perform

   a The next meeting will be _____ on 2nd March.
   b They're _____ their 25th wedding anniversary.
   c A soldier must _____ orders without question.
   d He enjoys _____ magic tricks at children's birthday parties.

4 bargain   discount   offer   sale

   a There's a(n) _____ of 20% on all cameras this week.
   b It was on special _____ – that's why I only paid £10 for it.
   c Wait until the _____ start before you go shopping for clothes.
   d I got a real _____ – these shoes were half price!

14

Word formation · verb → noun

12 Use the word in capitals to form a word that fits in the gap.

1 The police had to let him go because they had no _____ that he had committed a crime. — **PROVE**

2 Have you come to any _____ about the court case yet? — **CONCLUDE**

3 Being a police officer can be quite a dangerous _____ . — **OCCUPY**

4 When Philip graduated, he became a professional _____ . — **PHOTOGRAPH**

5 She had to have an _____ on her broken ankle. — **OPERATE**

6 We didn't realise the _____ of the news at the time. — **SIGNIFY**

7 The judge gave her a short sentence because she was a first-time _____ . — **OFFEND**

8 The high crime rate in the area influenced our _____ to move to the country. — **DECIDE**

Sentence transformation

13 Complete the second sentence so that it has a similar meaning to the first sentence, using the word given. Do not change the word given. You must use between two and five words.

1 She always has her hair cut by her aunt.

GETS

She always _____ her hair.

2 Our grass needs cutting this weekend.

CUT

We should _____ this weekend.

3 Somebody will remove your plaster tomorrow.

REMOVED

You _____ tomorrow.

4 I saw Lucas vandalise a bus shelter and now I don't like him anymore.

PUT

Seeing Lucas vandalise a bus shelter _____ him.

5 You'll get put in prison for a long time.

AWAY

They'll _____ for a long time.

6 The jury decided that the suspect did not commit the crime.

INNOCENT

The jury decided that the suspect _____ the crime.

7 After a few months in prison, he started behaving completely differently.

WAYS

After a few months in prison, he _____ completely.

8 Someone will deal with this problem tomorrow.

SEEN

I'll get this problem _____ tomorrow.

Unit 15

Awareness

1 **Which of these sentences are correct (C) and incorrect (I)?**

1 If you'll fall off your bike, you'll hurt yourself. ___

2 If you climb to the top, you'll be able to see the sea. ___

3 I won't put her in the team unless she'll train harder. ___

4 I'd buy the coat if I thought it suited me. ___

5 She wouldn't shout so much if she would behave herself. ___

6 If he hadn't missed his flight, he wouldn't have had to buy another ticket. ___

7 If you would have had a map, you wouldn't have got lost. ___

8 If I was you, I'd apologise immediately. ___

9 If you boil water, it would turn into steam. ___

10 Don't tell Wendy about the party if she phones. ___

How many did you get right? ☐

Grammar

Zero conditional

If clause	Main clause
present simple	present simple

We use the zero conditional to talk about an action that always / usually happens or a situation that is always true. We can use *when* instead of *if*.
If you **burn** fossil fuels, you **pollute** the atmosphere.
When you **burn** fossil fuels, you **pollute** the atmosphere.

First conditional

If clause	Main clause
present simple / continuous	*will* + infinitive

We use the first conditional to talk about the results of an action or situation that will probably happen now or in the future.
If the volcano **erupts**, *the village* **will be destroyed**.
If the climate **gets** *warmer, the sea level* **will rise**.

We can use *can, could, may* or *might* in the main clause instead of *will*. We can also use an imperative.
If you **want** *to be more environmentally friendly, you* **could** *install solar panels.*
If you **don't want** *to buy a drink,* **bring** *your own.*

Second conditional

If clause	Main clause
past simple / continuous	*would* + infinitive

We use the second conditional to talk about an action or a situation:
• that isn't true now.
If **I had** *the time,* **I would write** *a book.*
• that is unlikely in the future.
If everyone **stopped** *using plastic, fewer sea animals* **would die**.

We can also use the second conditional to give advice.
If I **were** *you, I'd buy an electric car.*

> **Note**
> We usually use *were* for all persons in second conditional sentences.
> *If Dan* **were** *here, he'd choose the vegetarian option.*

We can use *could* or *might* in the main clause instead of *would*.
You **could** stay in an eco-lodge if you **went** to Costa Rica.
I **might be able to** afford it if I **worked** through the summer.

Third conditional

If clause	Main clause
past perfect simple / continuous	*would* + *have* + past participle

We use the third conditional to imagine past events or situations that didn't actually happen. These are always hypothetical things because we cannot change the past.
*If my dad **had gone** to university, he **would have been** a geologist.* (He didn't go to university, so he isn't a geologist.)

We can use *could* or *might* in the main clause instead of *would*.
*We **could have helped** you if we **hadn't been** on holiday.*
*If the meeting **had been** earlier, I **might have been** there.*

Grammar exercises

2 **Choose the correct option to complete the sentences.**

1 If you are caught speeding, you *would get / get* a fine.
2 She *would / will* pass the exam if she studies hard.
3 Simon *didn't damage / wouldn't have damaged* the car if he had been more careful.
4 Unless we *put / don't put* the recycling in the right bin, they won't collect it.
5 If we *took / are taking* the bus instead of driving, it would help the environment.
6 If the baby *is / were* a girl, I'll call her Emily.
7 Sally *would be / is* very happy if she were offered the job.
8 She could have played football professionally if she *moved / had moved* to the USA.

3 **Complete the sentences with the first conditional.**

1 If I _____ (find) your notebook, I _____ (give) it to you.
2 If you _____ (not / know) the meaning, you _____ (look) in a dictionary.
3 We _____ (go) for a picnic if the weather _____ (be) nice tomorrow.
4 They _____ (not / believe) you even if you _____ (tell) them the truth.
5 I _____ (wash) the dishes if you _____ (be) tired.
6 We _____ (not / get) any festival tickets unless we _____ (go) earlier.
7 If the dog _____ (not / stop) barking, they _____ (call) the police.
8 She _____ (not / come) to the party if you _____ (not / invite) her.

4 Complete the sentences with the second conditional.

1 She would like to buy a new hybrid car, but she doesn't have enough money.

If she _____ enough money, she _____ a new hybrid car.

2 He eats a lot of red meat; that's why he's so unhealthy.

If he _____ a lot of red meat, he _____ so unhealthy.

3 She doesn't own a bike; that's why she can't cycle to work.

She _____ to work if she _____ a bike.

4 I get up late every morning, so I am always late for school.

I _____ late for school if I _____ late every morning.

5 He doesn't have much free time, so he doesn't see his friends very often.

If he _____ more free time, he _____ his friends more often.

6 They play loud music every night; that's why we can't sleep.

If they _____ loud music every night, we _____ .

5 Complete the sentences with the third conditional.

1 If they _____ (plant) more trees, the area _____ (not / flood) so easily.

2 If I _____ (know) that there was a recycling bank here, I _____ (bring) my old clothes.

3 If I _____ (see) you at the bus stop, I _____ (offer) you a lift.

4 I _____ (call) you if I _____ (not / lose) your telephone number.

5 We _____ (not / take) a taxi if the buses _____ (not / be) on strike.

6 They _____ (go) to the beach if it _____ (not / rain).

6 Complete the second sentence so that it has a similar meaning to the first.

1 Don't drive so much and you will help the environment.

If you _____ .

2 Can I borrow your bike? I can give it back to you this afternoon.

If you _____ .

3 Julia can't drink coffee because she gets a headache.

When _____ .

4 Why don't you talk to her about your problem?

If I were you, _____ .

5 Dan was thirsty because he left his water bottle in the park.

If Dan _____ .

6 I was listening to music, so I didn't hear my phone ring.

If I _____ .

7 Complete the sentences with one word in each gap.

1 I wouldn't be so confident if I _____ him.

2 She would _____ been happier if she had moved out of the city.

3 Martin doesn't travel by plane because it _____ bad for the environment.

4 _____ I had your email address, I'd send you the photo.

5 If I have enough time, I _____ come and visit you – but I can't be sure.

6 When you put salt on ice, _____ melts.

7 I won't call him if he _____ still working.

8 If more people use solar energy, it _____ become cheaper.

15

Vocabulary

Phrasal verbs

8 Match the phrasal verbs (1–8) with their meanings (a–h).

1	add to	☐	**a**	make something fall by using a sharp tool at its base
2	block out	☐	**b**	stop light or noise passing through
3	blow over	☐	**c**	persuade someone to do something
4	blow up	☐	**d**	increase the size, number or amount of something
5	cut down	☐	**e**	destroy with an explosion
6	slow down	☐	**f**	go or make something go less quickly
7	talk into	☐	**g**	take all of something so there is nothing left
8	use up	☐	**h**	(of a storm or argument) end without causing harm

9 Complete the sentences with the correct form of the phrasal verbs from Exercise 8.

1 We were lucky that the storm _____ quickly.

2 It wasn't easy, but I finally _____ my parents _____ buying me an electric scooter.

3 Burning fossil fuels _____ the problem of climate change.

4 If we eat less meat, we will _____ less land for farming.

5 I need some thick curtains to _____ the sunshine in the morning.

6 They _____ the tower block to destroy it, because it was unsafe.

7 Using energy from the sun or wind will help _____ the rate of climate change.

8 If we _____ our rainforests, many species of plants and animals will disappear.

Prepositions

10 Choose the correct option to complete the sentences.

1 Unfortunately, this tiny umbrella doesn't offer much protection *from / with / of* the rain.

2 It's very difficult to live with the threat *from / with / of* poverty every day.

3 I'm not sure that I can cope *from / with / of* not eating meat.

4 Is the customer satisfied *from / with / of* her new electric car?

5 The group is trying to make more people aware *from / with / of* climate change.

6 Don't let Simon discourage you *from / with / of* joining the club.

Collocations and expressions

11 Choose the correct option to complete the sentences.

1 We all need to *do / play* our bit to avoid single-use plastics.

2 Do you think having fines for *putting / dropping* litter would stop people doing it?

3 We need to *take / do* action to protect some natural habitats.

4 I hope that, one day, we can *put / make* an end to global poverty.

5 How do you think we can *drop / tackle* the problem of increasing carbon emissions?

6 Everyone can *make / play* a part in slowing down climate change.

Words easily confused

12 Complete the sentences with the correct form of these words. Use each word at least once.

1 | course   dessert   meal   starter |

   a Breakfast is the most important _____ of the day.

   b Apple pie and ice cream is my favourite _____ .

   c For the main _____ , I would like the vegan option, please.

   d I'll have soup for a _____ , please.

2 | aisle   corridor   line   now |

   a Why are you in the _____ when you should be in your classroom?

   b They live in a street with two neat _____ of identical bungalows.

   c I prefer a window seat to a(n) _____ seat when I'm flying.

   d Don't walk on the railway _____ .

   e The bride looked nervous as she walked down the _____ .

3 | consider   guess   reckon   wonder |

   a I _____ if Dad has already taken out the recycling.

   b Would you _____ switching to a renewable energy provider?

   c Can you _____ how many people there are in the world?

   d He _____ he lives a greener lifestyle than me.

4 | demonstration   display   exhibition   show |

   a Jim Jones has won first prize in the village flower _____ yet again.

   b It was the best firework _____ I have ever seen.

   c Can you give us a(n) _____ of how the machine works?

   d All the major manufacturers were represented at the technology _____ .

Word formation   verb or noun → adjective

13 Use the word in capitals to form a word that fits in the gap.

   1 This phone is completely _____ without a battery.   USE

   2 We watched a very _____ documentary about whales last night.   EDUCATE

   3 There has been a _____ increase in the amount of land used for agriculture.   DRAMA

   4 Some species of dolphin are _____ – there aren't many of them left.   DANGER

   5 The pollution from the factory is totally _____ – we need to campaign against it.   ACCEPT

   6 Many sea birds died as a result of the oil spill. It was an _____ disaster.   ECOLOGY

   7 Energy from the sun or the wind is known as _____ energy.   RENEW

   8 The technology works, but it's too expensive to use on a _____ scale at the moment.   MASS

Sentence transformation

14 Complete the second sentence so that it has a similar meaning to the first sentence, using the word given. Do not change the word given. You must use between two and five words.

1 The wall fell down because you didn't build it properly.

HAD

If _____ properly, it wouldn't have fallen down.

2 We won't finish this job without Rob's help.

US

If _____ , we won't finish this job.

3 It only works if you turn it on.

UNLESS

It _____ you turn it on.

4 My advice to you is to forget about it.

WERE

If _____ forget about it.

5 Molly was finally persuaded to come with us.

TALKED

We finally _____ with us.

6 I'm going to let the boss know about this.

AWARE

I'm going to _____ of this.

7 They want large organisations to stop using energy from fossil fuels.

PUT

They want to _____ large organisations using energy from fossil fuels.

8 We'll solve the problem more effectively if we all help.

BIT

We'll solve the problem more effectively if we all _____ .

Unit 16

Awareness

1 Which of these sentences are correct (C) and incorrect (I)?

1 Provided everyone agrees, we'll leave early. ___

2 If you hadn't told me, I still don't know. ___

3 She won't be able to help you otherwise she's busy. ___

4 As long it doesn't cost too much, I'll buy it. ___

5 Supposing we have some spare time, where shall we go? ___

6 If he hadn't taken the wrong road, he'd be here by now. ___

7 You are earning more money today if you had gone to university. ___

8 He'll do the work on condition that you pay him in advance. ___

9 I'm happy to come with you, provided my parents would give me permission. ___

10 Be quiet, otherwise you won't know what to do. ___

How many did you get right? [ ]

Grammar

Mixed conditionals

If clause	Main clause
past perfect simple / continuous	would + infinitive
or	
past simple / continuous	would + have + past participle

A mixed conditional is where the two clauses in a conditional sentence refer to different times. They contain one clause from a second conditional and one from a third conditional.
*If our car **hadn't been stolen** (a few hours ago), we**'d be** home in bed (now).*
*If they **cared** about the environment (now, in general), they **wouldn't have flown** to Edinburgh (last week).*

Conditionals without *if*

We can use *provided / providing that*, *on condition that* and *as long as* to replace *if* in first conditional sentences. These phrases mean *if* and *only if*.
***Provided that I have** the time, I**'ll come** and visit you this evening.*
*We**'ll go** to the beach tomorrow **on condition that** you **promise** to behave.*
***As long as** public transport is cheap, people **will use** it.*

We can use *unless* in first and second conditional sentences. It means the same as *if not*.
*She won't get to the meeting on time **if she doesn't get** a taxi.*
*She won't get to the meeting on time **unless she gets** a taxi.*

We can use *otherwise* to replace an *if* clause. It means *if not*.
***If you don't** drive more carefully, I'm not getting in the car with you.*
*Drive more carefully. **Otherwise**, I'm not getting in the car with you.*

We can use *suppose* or *supposing* in all conditional sentences, usually to ask questions. It means *imagine* or *what if*.
***Suppose / Supposing** you could live anywhere in the world, where would you choose?*
***Suppose / Supposing** we had run out of money, what would we have done?*

16

Grammar exercises

2 Complete the sentences with a mixed conditional.

1 If we _____ (not / miss) our flight, we would be lying in the sunshine right now.

2 You _____ (not / be) so tired now if you had gone to bed earlier.

3 If I didn't like chicken so much, I would _____ (become) a vegetarian years ago.

4 This town would still be beautiful if it _____ (not / be) polluted so badly.

5 If he didn't care about the environment, he _____ (not / install) solar panels.

6 If I _____ (have) a refillable water bottle, I would have brought it with me now.

3 Choose the correct option to complete the sentences.

1 *Provided / Unless / Otherwise* we have enough money, we'll buy an electric car.

2 Some species will become extinct *on condition that / unless / otherwise* we protect their habitats.

3 We'd better hurry up, *provided / unless / otherwise* we'll be late.

4 *As long as / Unless / Supposing* it rains tomorrow, the whole family is going on a picnic.

5 Steven agreed to wash my bicycle, *on condition that / unless / otherwise* I helped him with his maths.

6 *Provided / Unless / Supposing* you lost your job tomorrow, what would you do?

7 Carbon emissions will decrease *as long as / supposing / otherwise* we stop burning fossil fuels.

8 Let's not stay too long, *on condition that / otherwise / unless* we won't get home before dark.

4 Complete the second sentence so that it has a similar meaning to the first.

1 Some animals will lose their habitats if we don't eat less meat.
Unless _____ .

2 Don't call me if there isn't a problem.
Unless _____ .

3 We won't be able to sit together if we don't get on the boat now.
Unless _____ .

4 We won't go swimming if it isn't hot.
Unless _____ .

5 If you don't ask him, he won't help you.
Unless _____ .

6 This species will become extinct if we don't take action soon.
Unless _____ .

5 Complete the sentences with the correct form of the verbs.

1 Supposing you _____ (see) someone dropping litter, what would you do?

2 Supposing they hadn't wanted to fly, _____ they _____ (consider) the train?

3 Supposing there aren't any vegetarian options, what _____ you _____ (eat)?

4 Supposing she only _____ (travel) by public transport, how long will the journey take?

5 Supposing he hadn't got the job, what _____ he _____ (do) instead?

6 Supposing there _____ (be) a storm, where would they have found shelter?

6 Complete the sentences with one word in each gap.

1 Don't say anything to Sam about this _____ he asks you.
2 Yes, you can borrow my bike _____ long as you look after it.
3 _____ we use renewable energy, our carbon emissions will decrease.
4 He agreed to take the job on _____ that he could work at home twice a week.
5 They'd be safely home by now if they _____ got on that last bus.
6 Supposing I gave you the money – what _____ you spend it on?
7 You'd better not be late, _____ Jane will be furious.

Vocabulary

Phrasal verbs

7 Match the phrasal verbs (1–8) with their meanings (a–h).

1	freeze over	☐	a	tolerate
2	put up with	☐	b	(a surface of water) turn to ice
3	run out	☐	c	cause something to become extinct
4	soak up	☐	d	take in and hold water
5	take over	☐	e	use up or finish a supply of something
6	wear away	☐	f	take control
7	wear out	☐	g	make somebody feel very tired
8	wipe out	☐	h	make smaller or smoother over time

8 Complete the sentences with the correct form of the phrasal verbs from Exercise 7.

1 When our biology teacher was ill, the chemistry teacher _____ the class for a few days.
2 Forests are important in fighting climate change because they _____ carbon dioxide.
3 Because people used to take a shortcut over the field, they had _____ a path in the grass.
4 Many people are worried that tigers will be completely _____ by poachers.
5 We went skating on the lake, which had _____ during the night.
6 Unlike fossil fuels, wind and solar power won't _____ .
7 Tim moved to the countryside because he couldn't _____ the pollution in the city.
8 Elena was _____ because she had been working hard all day.

Prepositions

9 Choose the correct option to complete the sentences.

1 There has been a steep rise *in / on / to* the number of bicycle thefts in the area.
2 James is a very honest man – you can rely *in / on / to* him to tell you the truth.
3 It is important not to allow children to be exposed *in / on / to* too much violence in the cinema.
4 Does anyone object *in / on / to* the heating being turned down a bit?
5 Simone is really keen *in / on / to* saving the environment.
6 The decision to put more bins in the playground resulted *in / on / to* a reduction in the amount of litter.

16

Collocations and expressions

10 Complete the sentences with these words.

bee   cat   crocodile   fish   wolf   worm

1 When you manage to get someone to tell you something against their will, you _____ the information out of them.

2 When someone is pretending to be sad, we say that they are crying _____ tears.

3 A dangerous person who is pretending to be harmless is a _____ in sheep's clothing.

4 When you are trying to encourage people to say something nice about you, you _____ for compliments.

5 Someone who is working very hard is as busy as a _____ .

6 To let the _____ out of the bag means to accidentally reveal a big secret.

Words easily confused

11 Complete the sentences with the correct form of these words. Use each word at least once.

1   bar   lump   piece   sheet   slice

   a That's an interesting _____ of information.

   b Use a fresh _____ of paper for each question.

   c I'd like two _____ of ham in my sandwich.

   d How much sugar do you take, one _____ or two?

   e I've bought a _____ of chocolate for you.

2   income   interest   investment   salary

   a The bank pays _____ on my account twice a year.

   b As the managing director of a large company, she gets a large _____ .

   c His _____ consists largely of rent he receives from property he owns.

   d Buying shares in renewable energy wasn't considered a wise _____ at that time.

3   branch   compartment   department   ward

   a During my stay in hospital I shared a _____ with nine other patients.

   b The train was nearly empty, with only a few passengers in each _____ .

   c The local _____ of my bank has closed because more people are using internet banking.

   d He works for a government _____ , but I don't know which one.

4   earth   ground   land   soil

   a Sandy _____ is no good for growing these flowers.

   b I found the bracelet lying on the _____ outside.

   c Her family owns quite a lot of _____ .

   d What on _____ are you doing?

Word formation   adverbs

12 **Use the word in capitals to form a word that fits in the gap.**

1 We had a _____ awful holiday in Wales last winter.   **MEMORY**

2 The head teacher reacted _____ when he heard what Sam had done.   **FURY**

3 It's a pity they decorated the town centre so _____ – more people   **ATTRACTIVE**
   would visit if it looked nicer.

4 The dog quickly ate the food on the plate, and then looked _____ at   **GUILT**
   its owner.

5 The match ended _____ , with the losing team claiming that they   **CONTROVERSY**
   had been unfairly denied a penalty.

6 Stop behaving so _____ !   **FOOL**

7 The bus driver _____ steered the vehicle around the parked cars.   **SKILL**

8 The small boy _____ repeated the same question again and again,   **IRRITATE**
   until his mother finally told him to be quiet.

Sentence transformation

13 **Complete the second sentence so that it has a similar meaning to the first sentence, using the word given. Do not change the word given. You must use between two and five words.**

1 If you don't finish your dinner, you aren't allowed to watch TV.
   UNLESS
   You aren't allowed to watch TV _____ your dinner.

2 Supposing I hadn't been here to help you – what would you have done?
   IF
   What _____ I hadn't been here to help you?

3 If you promise to be home before midnight, you can go to the party.
   LONG
   You can go to the party _____ to be home before midnight.

4 Provided I can return it if I don't like it, I'll buy your computer.
   CONDITION
   I'll buy your computer _____ I can return it if I don't like it.

5 I'm not going to tolerate that loud music any longer.
   PUT
   I'm not going to _____ that loud music any longer.

6 I'll drive if you are feeling too tired to continue.
   OVER
   I'll _____ the driving if you are feeling too tired to continue.

7 I can't believe he revealed the secret on live TV!
   CAT
   I can't believe he _____ of the bag on live TV!

8 He's been looking after the children all day and now he's exhausted.
   WORN
   He _____ after looking after the children all day.

Part 1

For questions 1–8, read the text below and decide which answer (A, B, C or D) best fits each gap. There is an example at the beginning (0).

Take care, it's a jungle out there

The (0) __ of young children playing happily in the garden is a joy to behold, especially when parents believe that they can come to no (1) __ there. Parents will admit that children could be stung by a bee or scratch themselves on the rose bushes, but these are not (2) __ occurrences. In most people's (3) __ , being at home means staying safe.

Unfortunately, however, about four thousand British toddlers are poisoned by plants each year. Some of them have to (4) __ time in hospital because their condition is considered serious. Most parents are not (5) __ of which plants are poisonous. Often the flowers that are the most attractive are the most deadly, but it's no use trying to get this (6) __ to a small child!

Safety in the garden depends on parents paying close (7) __ to what their children are doing. When they are quiet, it often means they are (8) __ up to something. Leaving children unattended in the garden can be a risk.

0	(A) sight	B scenery	C view	D vision
1	A injury	B harm	C damage	D hurt
2	A common	B many	C often	D usual
3	A idea	B attitude	C opinion	D thought
4	A spend	B earn	C pay	D win
5	A aware	B knowing	C conscious	D learned
6	A back	B around	C into	D across
7	A notice	B attention	C attendance	D care
8	A breaking	B going	C getting	D staying

Part 2

For questions 9–16, read the text below and think of the word which best fits each gap. Use only one word in each gap. There is an example at the beginning (0).

A man with a vision

Stamford Raffles was born aboard a ship off the coast of Jamaica **(0)** _____*in*_____ 1781. Instead of attending university, he worked for the East India Company **(9)** _____ a clerk and studied hard in his spare **(10)** _____ . At the age of 30, he became governor of Java, where he employed zoologists and botanists **(11)** _____ discover all they could about the animals and plants on the islands. Raffles himself acquired a large collection of animals, including a Malayan sun bear that was brought up with his children. The bear often joined Raffles for dinner, eating fruit **(12)** _____ drinking champagne.

On a trip to Europe in 1817, Raffles had the idea for the forming of a collection of living animals. After founding the colony of Singapore in 1819, Raffles **(13)** _____ together with several influential scientists and aristocrats, **(14)** _____ listened carefully to his ideas. He convinced them, and he was voted president of **(15)** _____ Zoological Society of London. Raffles died suddenly in 1826. Sadly, the man whose idea it was to start London Zoo did not see its opening two years **(16)** _____ , in 1828.

Part 3

For questions 17–24, read the text below. Use the word given in capitals at the end of some of the lines to form a word that fits in the gap in the same line. There is an example at the beginning (0).

A holiday in Mauritius

With holiday resorts the world over getting more **(0)** _____*crowded*_____ , any place offering	CROWD
the opportunity of spending a holiday in a **(17)** _____ natural environment next	BEAUTY
to endless sandy beaches is guaranteed to be a major **(18)** _____ . But where	ATTRACT
is one to find such a paradise in this day and age? Mauritius, an almost perfectly circular island	
about 600 miles from the East African coast, can provide a wonderful, unspoiled location for just	
such a holiday. The island has very little **(19)** _____ at this point in its history.	TOUR
This means that **(20)** _____ today can enjoy its unspoiled scenery in relative calm,	VISIT
undisturbed by fellow holidaymakers. It is true that there are not many sights on the island, but	
(21) _____ is never a problem since local organisations offer exciting fishing and	BORE
sailing trips to **(22)** _____ areas where you can see some of the most breathtaking	HIDE
natural **(23)** _____ in the world. Mauritius is guaranteed to leave the holidaymaker	SCENE
(24) _____ relaxed.	COMPLETE

Part 4

For questions 25–30, complete the second sentence so that it has a similar meaning to the first sentence, using the word given. Do not change the word given. You must use between two and five words, including the word given. Here is an example (0).

Example:

0   You mustn't use a calculator in the test.

    ALLOWED

    You are _____ *not allowed to use* _____ a calculator in the test.

25   She is still making her decision.

    DECIDED

    She _____ to do yet.

26   I've only got a little luggage, so I don't need a trolley.

    MUCH

    I _____ luggage, so I don't need a trolley.

27   I am sure he has told her my secret.

    MUST

    He _____ my secret.

28   Some of the paintings are still for sale.

    BEEN

    Some of the paintings _____ yet.

29   They gave me a computer because I wanted to work at home.

    SO

    They gave me a computer _____ work at home.

30   The goods cannot leave the factory unless there is a signature on these papers.

    SIGNED

    These papers _____ the goods can leave the factory.

B2 Practice: ECCE

Grammar

For questions 1–20, choose the word or phrase that best completes the sentence.

1 If I ___ you, I wouldn't eat that much.
  A were
  B am
  C be
  D was

2 You will ___ shown to your room by this man.
  A be
  B being
  C have
  D having

3 We ___ new doors put in our house.
  A have had
  B have get
  C having
  D getting

4 If this car breaks down, we ___ be stuck here!
  A had
  B would have
  C will
  D can

5 ___ it rains tomorrow, what shall we do?
  A Providing
  B Supposing
  C Thinking
  D Imagining

6 You can wash the dishes, if you ___ to help.
  A are wanting
  B want
  C had wanted
  D would want

7 As ___ as you are happy, I am happy, too.
  A far
  B tall
  C long
  D wide

8 The bad news ___ given to my aunt yesterday.
  A is
  B was
  C were
  D are

9 He avoided ___ accused of fraud.
  A be
  B being
  C have
  D having

10 We hope ___ our new TV delivered today.
  A have
  B having
  C to have
  D had

11 He might be ___ to give you a lift.
  A can
  B able
  C how
  D want

12 You can't get in ___ you have a ticket.
  A unless
  B without
  C otherwise
  D would

13 We could ___ been the winners if we'd worked as a team.
  A of
  B had
  C would
  D have

14 We have to leave now, ___ we'll miss the bus.
  A unless
  B provided
  C otherwise
  D if

15 The boxer had his nose ___ in the fight.
  A broke
  B breaking
  C break
  D broken

16 I got my sister ___ my homework for me.
  A doing
  B to do
  C do
  D did

17 If you hadn't been sent off, we'd ___ holding that trophy now!
  A have
  B being
  C having
  D be

18 She'll do it, on ___ that you pay her.
  A situation
  B condition
  C provided
  D promise

19 They ___ all asked to participate.
  A be
  B were
  C have been
  D was

20 Look! I ___ my teeth whitened.
  A have
  B am having
  C have had
  D will get

Vocabulary

For questions 21–40, choose the word or phrase that most appropriately completes the sentence.

21 It's ___ the law to break the speed limit.
  A against
  B counter
  C versus
  D beside

22 I was in a deep sleep when my alarm went ___ .
  A in
  B out
  C off
  D on

23 She can see ___ your tricky scheme!
  A over
  B about
  C through
  D up

24 You can always rely ___ me to get the job finished.
  A of
  B on
  C for
  D to

25 The man turned out to be a wolf in ___ clothing.
  A dog's
  B cow's
  C goat's
  D sheep's

26 Are you ___ any suspicion for this crime?
  A with
  B under
  C over
  D beside

27 You should ___ yourself up to the police.
  A hold
  B put
  C give
  D take

28 I think it's time you ___ up to your crimes.
  A owned
  B showed
  C gave
  D turned

29 Mark will ___ over this project from now on, because I am giving up.
  A have
  B take
  C give
  D hold

30 The criminal was given a life ___ for murder.
  A jury
  B justice
  C service
  D sentence

31 Stop accusing me ___ cheating.
  A with
  B of
  C at
  D by

32 You can't do that – you're ___ the law!
  A breaking
  B making
  C taking
  D having

33 They had an argument, but it had ___ over by the evening.
  A blown
  B burst
  C gone
  D flown

34 We all play a(n) ___ in keeping our house tidy.
  A bit
  B part
  C end
  D action

35 That smell is really ___ me off my food.
  A getting
  B throwing
  C moving
  D putting

36 Two robbers ___ up a jewellery store in town.
  A took
  B held
  C brought
  D went

37 Let's go skating if the pond is frozen ___ .
  A out
  B hard
  C over
  D up

38 The woolly mammoth was ___ out during the Ice Age.
  A swept
  B brushed
  C cleaned
  D wiped

39 She won't be able to cope ___ such long hours!
  A on
  B after
  C with
  D at

40 I was talked ___ volunteering by my friends.
  A on
  B over
  C inside
  D into

Awareness

1 Which of these sentences are correct (C) and incorrect (I)?

1 She married a man her parents didn't approve of him. ___

2 I really like the car I bought last year. ___

3 Mr Fowler, that you met yesterday, is a famous author. ___

4 The singer you like is only 16 years old. ___

5 The printer that you bought it is faulty. ___

6 The story that I told you is untrue. ___

7 That's the place when I grew up. ___

8 Do you remember the time where we first met? ___

9 Eva, who was my babysitter years ago, has just got married. ___

10 Nobody knows the reason why it happened. ___

How many did you get right? ☐

Grammar

Relative clauses

Relative clauses give more information about a person, thing, place, etc. in a sentence. They are introduced by the following words:

- *who* for people
- *which* for things
- *whose* to show possession
- *when* for time
- *where* for places
- *why* for reason

Defining relative clauses

This type of relative clause gives us information that we need in order to understand who or what the speaker is talking about. We do not use commas to separate it from the rest of the sentence. We can use *that* instead of *who* and *which* in defining relative clauses.
*That's the café **where** I worked in the holidays.*
*We met some people **who / that** were very friendly.*

We often omit the relative pronoun from defining relative clauses, especially in informal English. But we can't omit it when it's the subject of the relative clause, and we never omit *whose*.
*The only exam (**which / that**) he didn't pass was French. (subject = he)*
*She's the other candidate (**who**) they interviewed for the job. (subject = they)*
*The person **who** answered the phone was very helpful. (subject = the person)*

Non-defining relative clauses

This type of relative clause gives us extra information which isn't necessary to understand the meaning of the main clause. We use commas to separate it from the rest of the sentence. We can't use *that* as the relative pronoun, and we can't omit the relative pronoun.
*My manager, **who wanted to start his own business**, left last week.*
*Her CV, **which we received yesterday**, is very impressive.*

Relative clauses with prepositions

When the relative pronoun is the object of a preposition, the preposition can come before *whom* (for people) or *which* (for things), but this is rather formal.
*This is the job advert **to which** I was referring.*
*The people **at whom** the course was aimed were mainly new managers.*

In everyday English, it's much more common to leave a short preposition in its original position, in which case the relative pronoun is often omitted from a defining relative clause.
*This is the job advert (**which / that**) I was referring **to**.*
*The people (**who / that**) the course was aimed **at** were mainly new managers.*

17

Grammar exercises

2 Choose the correct option to complete the sentences.

1 My mother was born at a time *when / which* her parents were working abroad.
2 Mrs Jenkins, *who / that* is sitting at the back of the hall, is the head teacher.
3 That's the man *which / that* I spoke to yesterday.
4 Mrs Black, *which / whose* husband also works here, is in charge of the company.
5 He didn't tell us the reason *why / which* he left his job.
6 The restaurant *which / where* we usually eat is the best in town.

3 Complete the sentences with a relative pronoun.

1 What is the name of the person _____ manages the volunteers?
2 The watch _____ I bought from your shop is not working anymore.
3 Does anyone know the reason _____ Liam didn't turn up for training today?
4 Is that the place _____ they are going to build the new office block?
5 That's the friend _____ mother is an electrician.
6 I'll never forget that summer _____ we all worked together.

4 Tick the sentences where the relative pronoun can be omitted.

1 Tim, whose sister won the tennis championship, is very happy. ___
2 The gift that my friend gave me for my birthday was really great. ___
3 I met a man whose mother is a famous musician. ___
4 Please return the book which I lent you. ___
5 This is the factory that they are going to knock down. ___
6 The supermarket where we usually shop is not too expensive. ___
7 The reason why I can't come to work is because I am unwell. ___
8 Anna, who travels a lot on business, has visited many countries. ___

5 Write sentences with a relative pronoun. Use commas where necessary.

1 Jenny is a successful lawyer. Her husband is unemployed.

_____

2 Sam has passed his driving test. He doesn't like taking the bus.

_____

3 Many people earn a lot of money. They work overtime.

_____

4 Mark runs a marketing company. He needs to find more clients.

_____

5 The Four Seasons Hotel is closing down. I stayed there for a week.

_____

6 The book is on the table. I have been looking for it.

_____

7 Last winter was a wonderful time for me. I worked in a ski resort.

_____

8 She wasn't honest in her CV. I really don't know the reason.

_____

6 Match the beginnings of the sentences (1–6) with their endings (a–f). Complete the sentences with a relative pronoun.

1 An employee is a person _____
2 A library is a building _____
3 J.K. Rowling is an author _____
4 A microscope is an instrument _____
5 1971 was the year _____
6 A pilot is a person _____

a books are stored.
b makes tiny things look bigger.
c the first email was sent.
d is paid to work for a company.
e books have sold millions of copies.
f flies a plane.

7 Complete the second sentence so that it has a similar meaning to the first sentence, using the word given. Do not change the word given. You must use between two and five words.

1 I met my wife in this place.
This _____ I met my wife. **WHERE**

2 That girl's mother is our doctor.
That's _____ is our doctor. **WHOSE**

3 We ate a delicious meal last night.
The meal _____ was delicious. **THAT**

4 I got a new laptop for my last birthday.
My last birthday _____ I got a new laptop. **WHEN**

5 He didn't get the job because he didn't prepare for the interview.
Not preparing for the interview _____ he didn't get the job. **WHY**

6 She volunteered there last year, and they offered her a job yesterday.
Yesterday they offered a job to the girl _____ last year. **WHO**

Vocabulary

Phrasal verbs

8 Match the phrasal verbs (1–8) with their meanings (a–h).

1 act as
2 cut down on
3 fill in
4 get down to
5 hold down
6 keep to
7 keep up
8 work on

a develop and improve
b keep a job
c reduce the number or amount of something
d start doing something properly
e continue
f complete a form
g stick with a plan
h do a job for a short time

9 Complete the sentences with the correct form of the phrasal verbs from Exercise 8.

1 Tim was never able to _____ a job for long because he was always late!
2 Please _____ this form and return it to the office as soon as possible.
3 Andrew is going to _____ office manager while Emma is away on holiday.
4 I need to _____ my time management skills before I ask for a promotion.
5 I'm trying to _____ our original plan, but some things have to be changed.
6 You're doing a great job – _____ the good work!
7 I think it's time we really _____ work on this project.
8 We're _____ the number of documents we print at work.

17

Prepositions

10 **Choose the correct option to complete the sentences.**

1 The city had been *over / through / under* attack for three days.
2 Ella's workspace isn't very tidy. There are papers all *over / through / under* her desk.
3 I often go for a run *over / through / under* the forest before work in the morning.
4 What time do you plan to pop *over / through / under* to my house this evening?
5 Don't worry. I have the situation *over / through / under* control.
6 Let me *over / through / under*! I'm a doctor.

Collocations and expressions

11 **Complete the sentences with the correct form of these verbs.**

get   give   go   make   miss   take

1 If his behaviour doesn't improve, he'll be _____ the sack.
2 She finally decided to _____ the initiative and phone her boss.
3 The workers decided to _____ on strike because they wanted more money.
4 Sarah worked until very late last night because she didn't want to _____ the deadline for her work.
5 Five people had to be _____ redundant because the company had lost money.
6 You're never going to _____ a promotion if you keep being late for work!

Words easily confused

12 **Complete the sentences with the correct form of these words. Use each word at least once.**

1 discover   find out   invent   set up

   a It was Marie Curie who _____ the chemical element radium.
   b Two brothers _____ the company 60 years ago.
   c One type of telescope was _____ by Sir William Herschel.
   d Can you _____ when the bus leaves, please?

2 allowance   pass   permission   permit

   a You need a(n) _____ to fish in this part of the river.
   b My parents give me a weekly _____ , which I use to buy food and clothes.
   c Our manager gave us _____ to come in later after we worked late the night before.
   d Please wear your _____ so that security can see it easily.

3 earlier   former   past   previous

   a As a(n) _____ prime minister, she has many important contacts.
   b We should have caught a(n) _____ flight.
   c How much _____ experience have you had?
   d She's not been well for the _____ few days.

4 fit   go with   match   suit

   a Red _____ both black and white.
   b If the jacket doesn't _____ , you can exchange it for a larger size.
   c Jeans don't really _____ him – he looks much better in smart trousers.
   d After buying a necklace, she searched for a pair of earrings to _____ .

Word formation   prefixes

13 Use the word in capitals to form a word that fits in the gap.

1 There must be some kind of _____ – we didn't order any food.   **UNDERSTAND**
2 Where did you _____ to earlier? You missed the meeting.   **APPEAR**
3 Try not to be so _____ – some people work more slowly than others.   **PATIENT**
4 That was the most _____ magic trick I have ever seen.   **CREDIBLE**
5 It took decades to _____ the city after the earthquake.   **BUILD**
6 Simon has been _____ ever since losing his job at the factory five years ago.   **EMPLOY**
7 I have arranged to _____ the loan, starting with £100 per month.   **PAY**
8 In spite of his mother's _____ , Mario decided to apply for a job as a stunt pilot.   **APPROVE**

Sentence transformation

14 Complete the second sentence so that it has a similar meaning to the first sentence, using the word given. Do not change the word given. You must use between two and five words.

1 She played her first professional football match in this stadium.
   WHERE
   This is _____ her first professional football match.

2 She had an interview for a job in a summer camp yesterday.
   WAS
   The interview _____ for a job in a summer camp.

3 You didn't get the job because you dressed too informally.
   REASON
   The _____ get the job was because you dressed too informally.

4 That dog's owner is a police officer.
   WHOSE
   That's _____ is a police officer.

5 We're trying to reduce the amount of electricity we use in the office.
   DOWN
   We're trying to _____ the amount of electricity we use in the office.

6 I'm going to start work on my novel properly this summer.
   GET
   This summer, I'm _____ work on my novel.

7 They dismissed him from his last job.
   SACK
   He _____ from his last job.

8 The factory workers have decided to stop working in protest against their working conditions.
   GO
   The factory workers have decided _____ in protest against their working conditions.

Awareness

1 Which of these sentences are correct (C) and incorrect (I)?

1 I found the boy hiding behind the sofa. ___
2 The girl was awarded first prize cried. ___
3 Having saw the film before, I didn't go with my friends to the cinema. ___
4 Walking home last night, my phone's battery went dead. ___
5 Not knowing what to do, I emailed you. ___

6 Seen from a distance, the insect looked green. ___
7 Looked through the window, I saw something move. ___
8 The man speaks at the moment is my uncle. ___
9 Having had a long holiday, my desk was full. ___
10 Having chosen the colours for her room, she went out to buy the paint. ___

How many did you get right? ☐

Grammar

Reduced relative clauses

When the relative pronoun is the subject of the relative clause, we can often reduce the relative clause (i.e. make it shorter) by using a present participle (verb + -ing) or past participle (verb + -ed or irregular form). The present participle has an active meaning; the past participle has a passive meaning. We can reduce both defining and non-defining relative clauses in the same way.
Everyone **who works** in the building must carry their security pass.
Everyone **working** in the building must carry their security pass.
I work in a building **which is known** as 'The Gherkin'.
I work in a building **known** as 'The Gherkin'.

The advantage of reduced relative clauses is that you can express your meaning in fewer words. The disadvantage is that the reader or listener has to work harder to work out the missing information, so you should only use them when the meaning is clear.

Participle clauses

Participle clauses are very similar to reduced relative clauses, but we use them for different purposes. They can start with a present participle (verb + -ing) or a past participle (verb + -ed or irregular form). We can use participle clauses to make sentences shorter. They can replace the subject and the verb in a sentence if the subject of both clauses is the same. We use a present participle if the verb is active and a past participle if the verb is passive. Participle clauses can replace full clauses with a range of conjunctions, including because, after, when and if.
Wanting his CV to stand out, Zak printed it on yellow paper. (= Because he wanted ...)
Asked what she thought, Kate said they should take on an assistant. (= After / When she was asked ...)
Given the chance, I'd travel and work abroad for a year. (= If I were given ...)

Because the reader or listener has to work harder to understand the missing information, you should only use participle clauses when the meaning is clear. We can make a participle clause negative by adding not.
Not understanding the question, I asked the interviewer to repeat it.

Perfect participle clauses

We can use a perfect participle (having + past participle) to combine clauses that have the same subject:
- when one action is completed before another action.
He had arrived early, so he had a coffee.
Having arrived early, he had a coffee.

- when one action has been going on for a period of time before another action starts.
She had been acting as office manager for three months, so she asked for a promotion.
Having acted as office manager for three months, she asked for a promotion.

The perfect participle can be used for active and passive sentences.
- active: having + past participle **Having sent** the email, she waited for a reply.
- passive: having been + past participle **Having been made redundant**, he was looking for a job.
We can make a perfect participle clause negative by adding not or never at the beginning.
Not / Never having created a CV before, he asked for advice.

Grammar exercises

2 **Choose the correct option to complete the sentences.**

1 *Checking / Check* the website that morning, Ben saw an interesting job advert.
2 *Having spoken / After spoken* to her manager, she applied for the position.
3 Students *wishing / wished* to take part in the careers fair must put their names down by the end of the week.
4 I'm interested in buying the car *advertising / advertised* on your website.
5 *Not being / Not been* able to speak German, I asked Rudi to translate for me.
6 The woman *interviewing / who interviewing* you was my aunt!

3 **Complete the sentences with the correct form of these verbs.**

call   live   offer   send   steal   study

1 A lot of the artwork _____ in to our studio last week was excellent.
2 She was delighted when she received a letter _____ her the job.
3 Police are looking for a car _____ from the car park last night.
4 A flood warning has been sent out to people _____ near the river.
5 Someone _____ Jacob left a message for you.
6 Every pupil _____ languages in this school has the opportunity to spend a month abroad.

4 **Rewrite the sentences using a present participle clause.**

1 Because I knew the traffic would be bad, I went by train.

_____

2 I'm not afraid of heights, so I don't mind climbing mountains.

_____

3 While Christine was walking through the park, she thought about life in France.

_____

4 Because we didn't want to disturb the meeting, we waited outside.

_____

5 I thought the dog might be hungry, so I gave it one of my sandwiches.

_____

6 She didn't know David's phone number, so she couldn't contact him.

_____

5 **Rewrite the sentences using a past participle clause.**

1 This song, which was written in the 1960s, remains one of the band's most popular.

_____

2 The politician didn't know what to say when he was asked about the economy.

_____

3 I would have been able to finish the exam if I had been given more time.

_____

4 The man who was wanted by the police got on a plane to Brazil.

_____

5 People all over the world admired Justin, but he didn't really like being famous.

_____

6 The cat felt safe and happy because it was hidden under a pile of cushions.

_____

6 **Rewrite the sentences using a perfect participle clause.**

1 As he had had a long holiday, Martin felt quite refreshed.

_____

2 After we had made the arrangements for the conference, we had lunch.

_____

3 Since I hadn't seen the presentation, I couldn't comment on it.

_____

4 After she had decided when she wanted to go, she bought her tickets.

_____

5 Because he hadn't had a bath for a couple of days, he felt dirty.

_____

6 As we had heard the news already, we weren't taken by surprise.

_____

Vocabulary

Phrasal verbs

7 **Match the phrasal verbs (1–8) with their meanings (a–h).**

1	move on	☐	a	employ
2	pick up	☐	b	learn
3	stand out	☐	c	start something new
4	take off	☐	d	remove money from your bank account
5	take on	☐	e	be easy to see or notice
6	take out	☐	f	have a short holiday
7	take round	☐	g	fill an amount of time or space
8	take up	☐	h	walk around a place with somebody to show it to them

8 **Complete the sentences with the correct form of the phrasal verbs from Exercise 7.**

1 Redecorating the office _____ the whole weekend.

2 She's been working here for too long, and now thinks it's time to _____ .

3 I'd like to _____ Monday _____ because I'll be studying all weekend.

4 The beach café is _____ extra staff during the summer.

5 Max, will you _____ Eva _____ the office, please?

6 How much money did you _____ this morning?

7 What can I do to make my CV _____ from everyone else's?

8 I didn't study Spanish – I _____ it _____ when I worked in Spain.

Prepositions

9 **Choose the correct option to complete the sentences.**

1 We kindly ask that guests present their passports _throughout / towards / upon_ arrival.

2 Daniela feels a lot of anger _throughout / towards / upon_ her previous manager.

3 Araf had such a bad cold that he coughed _throughout / towards / upon_ the interview.

4 The new manager has a strange attitude _throughout / towards / upon_ the staff.

5 When she came back into the room, she had a big smile _throughout / towards / upon_ her face.

6 She worked at weekends _throughout / towards / upon_ her degree.

Collocations and expressions

10 **Complete the sentences with these words.**

brains	brush	chance	feet	luck	shoes

1 If you can think on your _____ , you can make decisions quickly when under pressure.
2 You can't paint everyone with the same _____ – everyone is different.
3 Do you have a minute? I'd like to pick your _____ about this job application.
4 Try to put yourself in the interviewer's _____ and think about the questions they might ask.
5 She would jump at the _____ of working abroad. She'd love it!
6 Knowing my _____ , the train will be late and I'll be late for my new job!

Words easily confused

11 **Complete the sentences with the correct form of these words. Use each word at least once.**

1 | current   draught   drought   flood |

   a There's a _____ in here. Please close the window.
   b Strong _____ make swimming here very dangerous.
   c _____ have become common after heavy rain.
   d _____ is always a problem in areas of little rainfall.

2 | advantage   benefit   exploitation   profit |

   a You shouldn't take _____ of her good nature.
   b We expect to make a large _____ on the deal.
   c The _____ of these workers has to stop.
   d Free life insurance is just one of the _____ offered by the company.

3 | demand   inform   instruct   order |

   a I wasn't _____ about any change to the schedule.
   b Who _____ a cheese and mushroom pizza?
   c All employees will be _____ in the art of self-defence.
   d The customer _____ to speak to the manager in person.
   e Whoever _____ the protestors to vandalise the buildings made a terrible mistake.

4 | agenda   calendar   catalogue   directory   list |

   a Have you included Liam on the guest _____ ?
   b Look up her telephone number in the _____ .
   c I'm sorry I missed the meeting – it wasn't in my _____ .
   d As this item is not on the _____ , we can't discuss it at this meeting.
   e If you want to see all our products, take a look at our online _____ .

18

Word formation   mixed → noun

12 Use the word in capitals to form a word that fits in the gap.

1 Whose _____ is it to book meeting rooms?   **RESPONSIBLE**

2 We stayed in all morning waiting for a _____ that never came.   **DELIVER**

3 It is a(n) _____ to be short if you are a basketball player.   **ADVANTAGE**

4 After working at the hospital for 30 years, Sue is looking forward to a
   happy _____ .   **RETIRE**

5 I'll be happy with your decision because I trust your _____ .   **JUDGE**

6 The manager has a very good _____ with the whole team.   **RELATE**

7 My sister loves maths. She wants to be a financial _____ .   **ANALYSE**

8 She is going to have to do something about her _____ if she wants **LAZY**
   to be a success in life.

Sentence transformation

13 Complete the second sentence so that it has a similar meaning to the first sentence, using the word given. Do not change the word given. You must use between two and five words.

1 I hate travelling by boat because I can't swim.

   ABLE

   Not _____ , I hate travelling by boat.

2 We bought some more oil because we had used it all.

   THE

   Having _____ , we bought some more.

3 We should employ more people to help us.

   TAKE

   We should _____ people to help us.

4 Will you show Luke the new building?

   ROUND

   Will you _____ the new building?

5 Anna is very good at making decisions under pressure.

   FEET

   Thinking _____ is something that Anna is very good at.

6 As soon as you arrive at the resort, you must pay the bill.

   UPON

   You must pay the bill _____ the resort.

1 Which of these sentences are correct (C) and incorrect (I)?

1 Harry told that he wouldn't be back before noon. ___

2 The head teacher told us that he had already made his decision. ___

3 She said that she had to go to bed early that night. ___

4 He asked me where did I live. ___

5 I told him that he had to look for a better job. ___

6 Mark said us that he had forgotten to book a table. ___

7 She told him to not go out of the house. ___

8 Sally told us that she had already paid the bill. ___

9 He asked me to stop. ___

10 Ian told that he didn't want me to help him. ___

How many did you get right? ☐

Grammar

Reported speech

When we report what someone said or thought in the past, the tenses used by the speaker usually change. This process is called backshifting.

Direct speech	Reported speech
present simple	**past simple**
'She **enjoys** reading,' he said.	He said (that) she **enjoyed** reading.
present continuous	**past continuous**
'He is **studying** geography,' she said.	She said (that) he **was studying** geography.
present perfect simple	**past perfect simple**
'They have **failed** their exams,' he said.	He said (that) they **had failed** their exams.
present perfect continuous	**past perfect continuous**
'We **have been working** in the library,' he said.	He said (that) they **had been working** in the library.
past simple	**past perfect simple**
'He **gave** a presentation,' she said.	She said (that) he **had given** a presentation.
past continuous	**past perfect continuous**
'I **was researching** my project,' she said.	She said (that) she **had been researching** her project.

Other changes in verb forms are as follows.

can	could
'She **can** speak five languages,' he said.	He said (that) she **could** speak five languages.
may	might
'He **may** be early,' she said.	She said (that) he **might** be early.
must	had to
'She **must** do her homework,' he said.	He said (that) she **had to** do her homework.
will	would
'They **will** go to Spain for a week,' she said.	She said (that) they **would** go to Spain for a week.

19

> **Note**
>
> **1** We often use the verbs *say* and *tell* in reported speech. We follow *tell* with an object.
> *Our teacher **said** we should revise for the test.*
> *Our teacher **told us** we should revise for the test.*
>
> **2** We can leave out *that*.
> *She **said (that)** she preferred chemistry to biology.*
>
> **3** Remember to change pronouns and possessive adjectives where necessary.
> *'**We** are revising for the test,' he said.* → *He said (that) **they** were revising for the test.*

Reasons not to use backshifting

Do not use backshifting with the following tenses and words: past perfect simple, past perfect continuous, *would*, *could*, *might*, *should*, *ought to*, *used to*, and *had better*.
*'**I'd never studied** Italian before.'* → *She said she **had never studied** Italian before.*
*'You **should** apply to university.'* → *He told me I **should** apply to university.*

We use backshifting with *mustn't* and *must* when they refer to obligation, but not when *must* refers to logical deduction.
Obligation: *'You **must** hand in your projects on Friday.'* → *He told us we **had to** hand in our projects on Friday.*
Logical deduction: *'It **must** be fun to study abroad.'* → *She said it **must** be fun to study abroad.*

Do not use backshifting when the reporting verb is in a present tense, including the present perfect.
*'We **have** a trip in **July**.'* → *I've already **told** you that we **have** a trip in July. (Not: We had)*

Don't use backshifting if you want to emphasise that you agree with a statement, and it's still true now.
*'Elsa **needs** to do her homework.'* → *Your teacher told me you **need** to do your homework, Elsa. (and I agree)*

Changes in time and place

When we report direct speech, there are often changes in words that show time and place, too.

Direct speech	Reported speech
now	then
today / tonight	that day / night
yesterday	the previous day / the day before
last week / month	the previous week / month the week / month before
tomorrow	the next day / the following day
here	there

Reported questions

When we report questions, changes in tenses, pronouns, possessive adjectives, time and place are the same as in reported statements. In reported questions, the verb follows the subject as in ordinary statements and we do not use question marks.

When a direct question has a question word, we use this word in the reported question.
*'**When did you decide** to study engineering?' he asked.*
*He asked me **when I had decided** to study engineering.*

When a direct question does not have a question word, we use *if* or *whether* in the reported question.
*'**Do you speak** Mandarin?' he asked.*
*He asked **if / whether I spoke** Mandarin.*

Reported requests and orders

When we report orders, we usually use *tell* + object + (*not*)
to + infinitive.
'Turn off the computer!'
He **told me to** turn off the computer.
'Don't forget your homework,' he said to the students.
He **told the students not to** forget their homework.

When we report a request, we usually use *ask* + object +
(*not*) *to* + infinitive.
'Can you give me the login details, please?' she asked.
She **asked me to give** her the login details.
(Also: *She asked **if I could give** her the login details.*)
'Please don't talk during the test,' he said.
He **asked us not to talk** during the test.

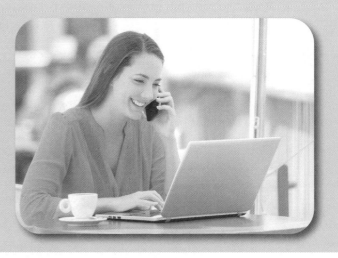

Grammar exercises

2 **Complete the sentences with the correct form of *say* or *tell*.**

1 She didn't _____ the teacher that she would be late.

2 He _____ that it was Maria's bag.

3 Tom _____ so many lies that nobody believes him anymore.

4 Sam _____ to me, 'I wasn't accepted by that college.'

5 He didn't _____ anything before he left.

6 Did Anna _____ you about the science competition?

3 **Choose the correct reported statement (a–b).**

1 'I got a job on an oil rig,' said Steven.

   a Steven said that he has got a job on an oil rig.

   b Steven said that he had got a job on an oil rig.

2 'I can't afford to go out again,' Sally said to me.

   a Sally told me that she couldn't afford to go out again.

   b Sally said me that she couldn't afford to go out again.

3 'I must do my homework now,' said Emily.

   a Emily said that she must do her homework then.

   b Emily said that she had to do her homework then.

4 'You left the computer switched on all night,' said Dad.

   a Dad said that I left the computer switched on all night.

   b Dad said that I had left the computer switched on all night.

5 He said to me, 'You explain things very clearly.'

   a He told me that I explained things very clearly.

   b He told me that I had explained things very clearly.

6 She said, 'We have been looking for images for two hours.'

   a She said that they had been looking for images for two hours.

   b She said that they were looking for images for two hours.

4 Complete the sentences with one word in each gap.

1 'I want to see your presentation today,' I said to her.

I told her that I _____ to see her presentation _____ day.

2 'I've missed the train. I'll be late,' said Beth.

Beth said that she _____ missed the train and she _____ be late.

3 Alice said, 'My teacher made me rewrite my essay yesterday.'

Alice said that her teacher _____ made her rewrite her essay the day _____ .

4 Piotr said, 'I am waiting for the results of my experiment.'

Piotr told me that he _____ waiting for the results of _____ experiment.

5 I said to my sister, 'I would like to borrow your laptop tomorrow.'

I told my sister that I would like to borrow _____ laptop the _____ day.

6 The professor said to us, 'I've marked your tests. I did it last night.'

The professor told us that she _____ marked our tests the _____ night.

7 Carol said to him, 'I need you to put the whiteboard here.'

Carol told him that she needed _____ to put the whiteboard _____ .

8 My mother said to my brother, 'You have to do your homework now.'

My mother told my brother that _____ had to do his homework _____ .

5 Rewrite the sentences in reported speech.

1 His mother said to us, 'He has been talking on the phone for an hour.'

_____

2 Ben said to Jen, 'I really don't feel ready to give my presentation tomorrow.'

_____

3 'I am trying to concentrate on my work now,' said John.

_____

4 'I can't find the file anywhere,' said Max.

_____

5 Her brother said to us, 'She'll come to your house when she has finished her homework.'

_____

6 'I haven't spoken to Jo since last month,' said Fiona.

_____

7 Her father said to her, 'You must revise for the exam today.'

_____

8 'I met an old friend of mine yesterday,' said Emily.

_____

6 **Complete the reported questions so that they mean the same as the direct questions.**

1 'When did Mr Brown leave the club?' asked the inspector.

The inspector asked _____ .

2 'Where's the tablet, Freddie?' asked Jessica.

Jessica asked Freddie _____ .

3 'What do you think happened?' enquired Zoe.

Zoe asked me _____ .

4 'Are you having a party on your birthday, Harry?' asked Toby.

Toby asked Harry _____ .

5 'Do you have a phone charger?' he asked me.

He wanted to know _____ .

6 'Why do you want to study here?' asked the interviewer.

The interviewer asked me _____ .

7 **Rewrite the orders and requests in reported speech.**

1 'Please don't mention it again,' he said to me.

_____

2 'Don't bite your nails,' she said to him.

_____

3 'Drink all your milk,' she said to her.

_____

4 'Stop complaining, please,' he said to me.

_____

5 'Don't lend Alex any money,' she said to me.

_____

6 'Don't be rude to our guests,' he said to me.

_____

7 'Tidy up your room, please,' she said to him.

_____

8 'Please follow me,' the guide said to us.

_____

Vocabulary

Phrasal verbs

8 **Match the phrasal verbs (1–8) with their meanings (a–h).**

1	breeze through	☐	a	quit a course of study
2	drop out	☐	b	succeed easily
3	fall through	☐	c	get an answer or result
4	get across	☐	d	fail to happen
5	get through	☐	e	succeed in making someone understand something
6	go through	☐	f	check something carefully
7	read through	☐	g	experience something difficult or unpleasant
8	work out	☐	h	come successfully to the end of a difficult time

9 Complete the sentences with the correct form of the phrasal verbs from Exercise 8.

1 Maria is _____ a difficult time at the moment.

2 He is so clever that he _____ every exam he takes.

3 Don't forget to _____ your essay to make sure there are no mistakes.

4 Matt _____ of university to start his own business.

5 I've finally _____ how this experiment works!

6 Eating and sleeping well will help you _____ your exams.

7 She's a great teacher – she _____ difficult ideas _____ really clearly.

8 I'm afraid the trip to London has _____ because the hotel is closed that week.

Prepositions

10 Choose the correct option to complete the sentences.

1 The doctor helped the child, even though she was *from / off / over* duty.

2 We had a geography trip to an island *from / off / over* the south coast.

3 Soon, the funny video was all *from / off / over* the internet.

4 Who knows what we'll be doing five years *from / off / over* now?

5 They spoke *from / off / over* the intercom, then she let him into the school office.

6 The teacher lets us have a longer break *from / off / over* time to time.

Collocations and expressions

11 Match the sentence beginnings (1–6) with their endings (a–f) to make definitions.

1 When you say you are brain dead, ☐   a you think about it all the time.

2 A brainwave is ☐   b is the person who had the idea.

3 If you brainstorm something ☐   c you all try to solve a problem or think of ideas together.

4 The brains behind something ☐   d you think very hard.

5 If you have something on your brain, ☐   e a sudden, unexpected idea.

6 When you rack your brains ☐   f you mean that you are too tired to think.

Words easily confused

12 Complete the sentences with the correct form of these words. Use each word at least once.

1 belong   own   possess

   a Who does this bag _____ to?

   b Do you know who _____ this coat? We found it on the school field.

   c For a person who _____ such skill, his work could be better!

2 danger   emergency   risk   urgency

   a According to the head teacher, it was a matter of _____ .

   b You can only use your phone in class in a(n) _____ .

   c Several employees are in _____ of losing their jobs.

   d Our teachers are very careful not to take _____ on school trips.

3 bunch   bundle   collection   packet

   a I always have a small _____ of grapes with my lunch.

   b We saw an amazing _____ of ancient artefacts in the museum.

   c They had found the old papers tied up in a _____ at the bottom of the drawer.

   d He threw his _____ of crisps away because they tasted strange.

4 | decrease   drop   lessen   lower |

a Please _____ your voice.

b Take some extra blankets in case the temperature _____ in the evening.

c The number of new students has _____ from 270 to 240.

d Don't use too much text – it _____ the impact of the image.

Word formation   mixed

13 **Use the word in capitals to form a word that fits in the gap.**

1 The teacher said our final _____ would be based on essays and exams. **ASSESS**

2 This is one of the _____ assignments I have ever done in my life. **TRICK**

3 Mr Bennett suggested that Maths Club would be _____ for me. **BENEFIT**

4 You will be asked to go home and change if you are not dressed _____ . **SUIT**

5 It's really _____ when you shout at the children like that – it only makes things worse. **HELP**

6 Penicillin was the most important medical _____ of the 20th century. **DISCOVER**

7 My brother has just finished university. We're going to his _____ ceremony next week. **GRADUATE**

8 Sam's mother is a famous _____ . **NOVEL**

Sentence transformation

14 **Complete the second sentence so that it has a similar meaning to the first sentence, using the word given. Do not change the word given. You must use between two and five words.**

1 'Please don't park here,' she said to me.

ASKED

She _____ park there.

2 He told the children not to run.

NOT

'Do _____ ,' he told the children.

3 'Where do you want to go tonight?' he asked us.

THAT

He asked us where _____ night.

4 Our teacher told us to listen to him.

ME

'_____ !' our teacher told us.

5 'I can help you fix that,' she said.

ME

She told me that she _____ fix that.

6 'Do you want to go to university?' the professor asked them.

IF

The professor asked _____ to go to university.

7 'I'm busy now,' she said.

WAS

She said she _____ .

Unit 20

1 Which of these sentences are correct (C) and incorrect (I)?

1 Thank you for agreeing help us. ___
2 I advise you not to spend all your money. ___
3 She reminded me buying some tomatoes. ___
4 He recommends to put it in the oven for 50 minutes. ___
5 I apologise for being so thoughtless. ___
6 The teacher accused him of copying. ___
7 She persuaded me go with her. ___
8 I promised taking them to the cinema. ___
9 They demanded that I bought them ice cream. ___
10 He was complaining about having to go to work so early. ___

How many did you get right? ☐

Grammar

Reporting verbs

As well as the verbs *say*, *tell* and *ask*, we can use other verbs to report what someone says more accurately. Notice the different structures.

verb + *to* + infinitive	
agree	'Yes, I'll fix it for you,' he said. He **agreed to fix** it for us.
claim	'I'm good at fixing things,' he said. He **claimed to be** good at fixing things.
decide	'I think I'll fix it,' he said. He **decided to fix** it.
offer	'Shall I fix it?' he said. He **offered to fix** it.
promise	'Don't worry, I'll fix it,' he said. He **promised to fix** it.
refuse	'I won't fix it,' he said. He **refused to fix** it.
verb + object + *to* + infinitive	
advise	'If I were you, I'd revise more,' she said. She **advised me to revise** more.
encourage	'Go on, revise more and you'll get better marks,' she said. She **encouraged me to revise** more.
order	'Revise!' she said. She **ordered me to revise**.
persuade	'You should revise more – you'll feel more confident,' she said. 'You're right!' I said. She **persuaded me to revise** more.
remind	'Don't forget to revise,' she said. She **reminded me to revise**.
warn	'Revise more – don't fail your exam,' she said. She **warned me not to fail** my exam.
verb + *-ing* form	
admit	'I lost your headphones,' he said. He **admitted losing** my headphones.
deny	'I didn't lose your headphones,' he said. He **denied losing** my headphones.
recommend	'You should buy new headphones,' he said. He **recommended buying** new headphones.
suggest	'Let's buy new headphones,' he said. He **suggested buying** new headphones.
verb + preposition + *-ing* form	
apologise for	'I'm sorry I broke your laptop,' she said. She **apologised for breaking** my laptop.
complain of / about	'I broke my laptop again,' she said. She **complained about breaking** her laptop again.
insist on	'Don't be silly. I'll buy a new laptop for you,' she said. She **insisted on buying** a new laptop for me.

verb + object + preposition + -*ing* form	
accuse someone of	'I'm sure you copied my answers,' he said. He **accused me of copying** his answers.
congratulate someone on	'You got all the answers right! Well done!' he said. He **congratulated me on getting** all the answers right.
verb + *that* **clause**	
announce	'I'm going to do it,' she said. She **announced that** she was going to do it.
complain	'I don't have time to do it,' she said. She **complained that** she didn't have time to do it.
demand	'You do it,' she said. She **demanded that** I do it.
verb + indirect question	
enquire	'Can I present first?' he asked. He **enquired whether he could** present first.
question	'Why do we need to arrive so early?' She **questioned why they needed to arrive** so early.
wonder	'What will university be like?' he asked. He **wondered what university would be** like.

Many reporting verbs can have more than one pattern.

She admitted **copying / that she had copied**.
She claimed **to be / that she was** …
She insisted **on / that she would** …
She promised **to / that she would** …
She recommended **going / that we should go** …

She reminded me **to / that I should** …
She suggested **taking / that we should take** …
She threatened **to / that she would** …
She warned me **not to / that I shouldn't** …

Grammar exercises

2 Choose the correct option to complete the sentences.

1 The head teacher *advised / suggested* me to apply to university.
2 The boy *apologised / admitted* breaking the window.
3 He *complained / refused* that he was tired.
4 My dad *congratulated / encouraged* me on winning the competition.
5 I'm surprised that he *denied / refused* to sign the papers.
6 The teacher *persuaded / demanded* them to sit down and work quietly.
7 I *accused / warned* my classmate of copying my work.
8 My sister *offered / reminded* me to take my tennis racket.

3 Complete the sentences with the correct form of the verbs.

1 She suggested _____ (eat) at the new restaurant.
2 The man denied _____ (steal) the laptop.
3 I was so glad that Dan agreed _____ (come) with us.
4 My tutor encouraged me _____ (enter) the competition.
5 Liz demanded that I _____ (drive) her home.
6 I apologised for _____ (not / remember) my sister's birthday.

4 Complete the sentences with one word in each gap.

1 He decided _____ move to Italy.
2 She advised _____ not to buy it, so I didn't.
3 I don't believe he accused you _____ lying.
4 What was she apologising _____ ? It wasn't her fault!
5 My dad insisted _____ paying the bill.
6 The teacher announced _____ there was going to be a test the next day.

5 Complete the sentences in reported speech using a suitable reporting verb.

1 'You took my phone and broke it,' he said to me.
He _____ .

2 'You should go to bed earlier,' she said.
She _____ .

3 'Don't forget to bring the things I asked for,' she said to me.
She _____ .

4 'I'm so sorry I damaged the bike,' the child said.
The child _____ .

5 'You hit Pablo with your bag,' said the teacher to Jake.
The teacher _____ .

6 'Leave the courtroom immediately,' the judge said to the jury.
The judge _____ .

6 Rewrite the sentences in direct speech.

1 Adam ordered Ben to be quiet, but Ben refused.
Adam: *'Be quiet.'* _____   **Ben:** *'No. (I won't.)'* _____

2 The twins asked Sophie to help them. Sophie agreed.
Twins: _____   **Sophie:** _____

3 Sara accused Tom of eating her sandwich. Tom denied it.
Sara: _____   **Tom:** _____

4 Mum reminded me to buy a present for Georgie. I thanked her.
Mum: _____   **Me:** _____

5 The doctor advised me to drink more water, and I agreed.
Doctor: _____   **Me:** _____

6 The police officer ordered the boy to get off his bike. The boy refused.
Police officer: _____   **Boy:** _____

Vocabulary

Phrasal verbs

7 Match the phrasal verbs (1–8) with their meanings (a–h).

1	go for	☐	**a**	say that someone has done something wrong
2	go over	☐	**b**	try to get
3	hand in	☐	**c**	look at again, revise
4	hand out	☐	**d**	submit work
5	look out for	☐	**e**	find information about
6	look up	☐	**f**	write something so you remember it later
7	note down	☐	**g**	distribute something among a group
8	tell off	☐	**h**	try to notice something or somebody

8 **Complete the sentences with the correct form of the phrasal verbs from Exercise 7.**

1 You might find it helpful to _____ the key points.
2 _____ Gina when you go to the conference. She said she was going.
3 I'm training very hard because this time I am _____ the gold medal.
4 The teacher _____ Mia _____ for answering her phone in class.
5 If you don't know what I'm talking about, _____ it _____ on the website.
6 He _____ the vocabulary list one more time before doing the test.
7 Your homework will not be marked if you _____ it _____ late.
8 The teacher _____ the worksheets to everyone in the class.

Prepositions

9 **Choose the correct option to complete the sentences.**

1 It's *against / after / along* the law to drive without a seatbelt on.
2 They never went on a school trip again *against / after / along* the way they behaved.
3 What do your parents think about you having a party in their house? Mine are *against / after / along* it.
4 The football pitch is just *against / after / along* the road from the school.
5 I knew all *against / after / along* that Stefan was not an honest person.
6 It turned out that we were going in the right direction *against / after / along* all.

Collocations and expressions

10 **Complete the sentences with *take*, *get* or *keep*.**

1 Susan _____ great pleasure in editing the school magazine.
2 I _____ the feeling that Theresa is going to leave her job soon – she seems very unhappy.
3 Would you like me to _____ you company on the journey home?
4 Let me _____ straight to the point – I don't think you are working hard enough.
5 I didn't know the sports centre was open on Sunday, but I'll _____ your word for it.
6 Dad _____ his promise to me and bought me a bicycle for my birthday.

Words easily confused

11 **Complete the sentences with the correct form of these words. Use each word at least once.**

1 comment   mention   notice   refer

  a Please don't _____ the party to Oscar – I didn't invite him.
  b He didn't _____ on your work at all.
  c I wish I hadn't _____ to my ambitions during the discussion.
  d The pickpocket was so quick that only one witness _____ what he was wearing.

2 only   separate   single   unique

  a Being a(n) _____ child, she had no brothers or sisters to play with.
  b It's a(n) _____ opportunity for you learn Spanish in Spain.
  c Are you married or _____ ?
  d Remember to keep your school shirts _____ from the others.

3 certificate   degree   licence   subject

  a History was the one _____ I was never good at.
  b I seem to have lost my birth _____ .
  c She has a _____ in architecture from Birmingham University.
  d This driving _____ is not valid in Canada.

4 adviser   coach   instructor   tutor

   a My driving _____ thinks I'm ready to take my driving test.

   b I hadn't thought of studying law until the careers _____ suggested it.

   c The team has improved so much with the new _____ .

   d Do you think a few English lessons with a private _____ would help?

Word formation   mixed

12 **Use the word in capitals to form a word that fits in the gap.**

   1 The teacher was concerned about one pupil's high rate of _____ . **ABSENT**

   2 It is not _____ to expect a young child to understand such complex maths. **REASON**

   3 I am writing in _____ to your recent podcast. **REFER**

   4 Everyone was surprised when our team won the _____ . **CHAMPION**

   5 I've got a test tomorrow, but I'm worried that I'll never _____ all my notes! **MEMORY**

   6 My lecturers have given me so much support and _____ . **ENCOURAGE**

   7 I'm so relieved – I've got my essay back and there are only a few _____ . **CORRECT**

   8 Greg was shocked at the _____ of the people – nobody spoke to him! **FRIENDLY**

Sentence transformation

13 **Complete the second sentence so that it has a similar meaning to the first sentence, using the word given. Do not change the word given. You must use between two and five words.**

   1 'OK, I'll give you a lift to the concert,' said Tom.

     TO

     Tom _____ us a lift to the concert.

   2 'Sit down!' she said to us.

     ORDERED

     She _____ down.

   3 'It's true, I forgot my homework,' Becky said.

     ADMITTED

     Becky _____ her homework.

   4 'I'm really sorry I hurt you,' he said to her.

     FOR

     He _____ her.

   5 'Well done! You won the competition,' he said to me.

     ON

     He _____ the competition.

   6 'Tell me how you discovered my password!' she said to me.

     THAT

     She demanded _____ how I discovered her password.

   7 'You lied to me,' she said.

     OF

     She _____ to her.

   8 'No, I won't do what you tell me,' he said to them.

     REFUSED

     He _____ they told him.

B2 Practice: First

Part 1

For questions 1–8, read the text below and decide which answer (A, B, C or D) best fits each gap. There is an example at the beginning (0).

Jailbirds

Although the therapeutic **(0)** ___ of pets has been appreciated for some time, they have not been permitted in British prisons until relatively **(1)** ___ . Not long ago it occurred to the prison authorities that prisoners serving long sentences must feel **(2)** ___ by society and that was the reason why they became less cooperative. It was then suggested that they were likely to respond positively if they were **(3)** ___ to keep a budgie. Realising that long-term prisoners go through a great deal of suffering, the appropriate government department went **(4)** ___ with the idea.

After a trial period, the authorities reached the conclusion that looking after a small, helpless bird brought out a **(5)** ___ side in most prisoners. This, in turn, **(6)** ___ some prisoners and their jailers closer together. The authorities were relieved because there had been some opponents to the scheme, who had passionately warned against it. Since the scheme was set up, inmates have been able to **(7)** ___ from the boredom of prison life and see their situation from a completely different **(8)** ___ .

0	**A** price	**B** cost	**C** value	**D** worth
1	**A** lately	**B** recently	**C** shortly	**D** soon
2	**A** abandoned	**B** vanished	**C** mislaid	**D** left
3	**A** allowed	**B** let	**C** left	**D** agreed
4	**A** across	**B** along	**C** down	**D** up
5	**A** sensitive	**B** sensible	**C** logical	**D** truthful
6	**A** fetched	**B** took	**C** brought	**D** carried
7	**A** prevent	**B** avoid	**C** block	**D** escape
8	**A** corner	**B** edge	**C** angle	**D** opinion

Part 2

For questions 9–16, read the text below and think of the word which best fits each gap. Use only one word in each gap. There is an example at the beginning (0).

Childhood obesity

The problem of obesity, **(0)** ___*which*___ refers to the excessive accumulation of body fat, is affecting more and more children in Western society **(9)** _____ days. It is estimated that about one in ten six-year-olds is obese. Meanwhile, figures in the United States suggest that up **(10)** _____ 30% of US children **(11)** _____ overweight.

Although very few health problems **(12)** _____ been observed in obese children so far, it is believed that they run a greater risk of developing conditions such **(13)** _____ high blood pressure or heart disease later in life. Already, the number of children suffering from type-2 diabetes, a serious illness that previously mostly affected middle-aged people, has gone **(14)** _____ .

Experts blame this weight problem **(15)** _____ unhealthy eating habits. These habits combined with the sedentary lifestyle of many children, **(16)** _____ spend hours in front of their computers or TVs, are responsible for most cases of obesity.

Part 3

For questions 17–24, read the text below. Use the word given in capitals at the end of some of the lines to form a word that fits in the gap in the same line. There is an example at the beginning (0).

Taking the blame

Among many other things, **(0)** _____*pollution*_____ is a sensitive political issue in many   **POLLUTE**

countries in the world today. All parties, not just the Greens, now include

(17) _____ policies in their election manifestos. As a result of this, one would   **ENVIRONMENT**

be forgiven for assuming that the amount of **(18)** _____ waste being released   **INDUSTRY**

is decreasing. However, the evidence suggests that this is very unlikely to be the case. In fact,

all the research to date shows that the **(19)** _____ of our environment is not   **DESTROY**

slowing down at all. It is a truly **(20)** _____ issue which requires international   **GLOBE**

cooperation to combat, and it appears that we are failing.

Many attempts have been made to **(21)** _____ the reasons for this. It is easy to   **IDENTITY**

point the finger at government ministers and business people, and it does appear that many of

them are behaving **(22)** _____ . But it could be argued that putting the blame   **RESPONSIBLE**

on these people simply gives the general public licence to continue **(23)** _____   **GREEDY**

consuming the very products which are causing such devastating damage to the environment.

If the public's **(24)** _____ was more positive and well-informed, perhaps the   **RESPOND**

situation would change for the better.

Part 4

For questions 25–30, complete the second sentence so that it has a similar meaning to the first sentence, using the word given. Do not change the word given. You must use between two and five words, including the word given. Here is an example (0).

Example:

0 It isn't necessary for you to go to every lesson.

ATTEND

You _____ *needn't / don't need to attend* _____ every lesson.

25 The president found what the manager said embarrassing.

EMBARRASSED

The president _____ comments.

26 Her brother didn't have nearly as much success in the job as she did.

MORE

She did the job _____ her brother.

27 A famous architect is designing a house for them.

DESIGNED

They _____ by a famous architect.

28 He started his stamp collection about 20 years ago.

COLLECTING

He _____ about 20 years.

29 I'd rather work here than get a job in the city.

PREFER

I _____ a job in the city.

30 Liz often forgets to switch on the alarm.

TIME

It's not the _____ to switch on the alarm.

B2 Practice: ECCE

Grammar

For questions 1–20, choose the word or phrase that best completes the sentence or conversation.

1 Julia ___ that she'd be back soon.
   A said
   B told
   C asked
   D talked

2 Mrs Smith, ___ I thought was on holiday, is here.
   A which
   B that
   C who
   D she

3 He apologised ___ being late.
   A for
   B to
   C of
   D with

4 The police officer ___ ride on the pavement.
   A told me to not
   B told me not to
   C said me not to
   D said me to not

5 The woman ___ at the moment is my mum.
   A speaking
   B speaks
   C to speak
   D speak

6 ___ being able to dance, I don't enjoy parties.
   A No
   B None
   C Not
   D Can't

7 ___ from the air, the patterns are quite beautiful.
   A Seeing
   B See
   C Saw
   D Seen

8 Not wanting ___ rude, I sat quietly until the end of the meal.
   A being
   B be
   C was
   D to be

9 Why did you insist ___ early?
   A to leave
   B on leaving
   C leaving
   D on leave

10 Did he ___ if you were OK?
   A say
   B tell
   C ask
   D talk

11 Do you know the reason ___ it happened?
   A how
   B when
   C which
   D why

12 I asked her ___ she would like to have dinner.
   A whether
   B that
   C may
   D could

13 ___ heard the music, I didn't download it.
   A Being
   B Having
   C Doing
   D Making

14 Greta decided ___ at home.
   A stay
   B staying
   C stayed
   D to stay

15 I'm furious! He accused me ___ !
   A to cheat
   B of cheating
   C cheating
   D cheat

16 Our house, ___ we bought in 2015, is for sale.
   A which
   B what
   C who
   D it

17 'Why didn't Dan want to eat anything?'
   'He said he ___ dinner.'
   A already has
   B had already
   C has already has
   D had already had

18 I recommend ___ to see this play.
   A to go
   B of going
   C going
   D go

19 That's the girl ___ dad is the new head teacher.
   A which
   B who's
   C that's
   D whose

20 This is ___ I sleep.
   A room
   B where
   C bed
   D place

Vocabulary

For questions 21–40, choose the word or phrase that most appropriately completes the sentence.

21 Could you ___ in this application form, please?
   A   put
   B   fill
   C   hold
   D   write

22 I knew who the killer was all ___ .
   A   against
   B   after
   C   along
   D   away

23 She ___ through her final exams easily.
   A   blew
   B   ran
   C   breezed
   D   whistled

24 Have you ___ out how to do it yet?
   A   stood
   B   dropped
   C   handed
   D   worked

25 Why don't you ___ the initiative and contact the company?
   A   keep
   B   make
   C   take
   D   get

26 Playing computer games ___ up too much of your time.
   A   makes
   B   takes
   C   spends
   D   holds

27 Do you think you'll still be here five years ___ now?
   A   by
   B   from
   C   out
   D   away

28 I've worked here long enough. I think it's time to ___ on.
   A   go
   B   make
   C   move
   D   leave

29 I'll pop ___ to your house this evening.
   A   after
   B   under
   C   through
   D   over

30 The sun shone ___ the weekend.
   A   in
   B   throughout
   C   out
   D   within

31 I had to think on my ___ when they asked me a question I wasn't expecting.
   A   feet
   B   shoes
   C   brains
   D   luck

32 He ___ at the chance of working from home.
   A   jumped
   B   kicked
   C   put
   D   got

33 There is litter ___ over the place!
   A   every
   B   all
   C   some
   D   around

34 Keep ___ the good work, Jerry!
   A   up
   B   down
   C   on
   D   off

35 May I ___ your brains about this project?
   A   pick
   B   rack
   C   kick
   D   pack

36 You ___ up the language very quickly.
   A   lifted
   B   got
   C   took
   D   picked

37 Look ___ for the traffic wardens around here!
   A   out
   B   up
   C   over
   D   along

38 Do you ever ___ the feeling that you're being watched?
   A   take
   B   make
   C   hold
   D   get

39 It was boring with nobody to ___ me company.
   A   give
   B   hand
   C   keep
   D   bring

40 Their plans to travel round Europe fell ___ when their van broke down.
   A   through
   B   down
   C   over
   D   off

Unit 21

Awareness

1 Which of these sentences are correct (C) and incorrect (I)?

1 My new phone is most expensive than yours. ___
2 The weather is too hot today. ___
3 Your test results weren't enough good. ___
4 This cartoon isn't as funny as the last one. ___
5 The higher you climb, the more you see. ___
6 You'll get there more quick if you cycle. ___

7 She gave the toy to the child who asked the most politely. ___
8 That dress is such gorgeous. ___
9 This is the worst photography exhibition I've ever seen. ___
10 The weather was so bad that we didn't leave our hotel. ___

How many did you get right? ☐

Grammar

Comparative and superlative structures

We use the comparative to compare two people or things. We usually form the comparative by adding -er to an adjective or adverb. If the adjective or adverb has two or more syllables, we use the word *more*. We often use the word *than* after the comparative.
*Taking the train is **cheaper than** flying.*
*The bus goes **more frequently than** the train.*

We use the superlative to compare one person or thing with other people or things of the same type. We usually form the superlative by adding -est to the adjective or adverb. If the adjective or adverb has two or more syllables, we use the word *most*. We usually use the word *the* before the superlative.
*What is **the longest** mountain range in the world?*
*I understood Carlos because he spoke **the most slowly** of all the people in the group.*

Spelling: hot → ho**tt**er / ho**tt**est, brave → brav**er** / brav**est**, tiny → tin**ier** / tin**iest**

Some adjectives and adverbs are irregular and form their comparative and superlative in different ways.

Adjective / Adverb	Comparative	Superlative
good / well	better	the best
bad / badly	worse	the worst
far	farther / further	the farthest / furthest

Other comparative structures

We use *as* + adjective / adverb + *as* to show that two people or things are similar in some way.
*Do you think self-catering cottages are **as comfortable as** hotels?*

We use *not as* / *so* + adjective / adverb + *as* to show that one person or thing has less of a quality than another.
*New York isn't **as polluted as** Los Angeles.*

We use *less* / *the least* + adjective / adverb to mean the opposite of *more* / *the most*.
*The resort is **less crowded** than it used to be. (= It's emptier.)*
*This hotel is one of **the least expensive** in the area.*

We use *the* + comparative, *the* + comparative to show that as one thing increases or decreases, another thing is affected.
***The warmer** the weather, **the higher** the number of people on the beach.*

Intensifiers

We can use *much, far, a lot* or *considerably* before a comparative to make the meaning stronger.
*The pool is **considerably hotter** than the sea.*

We can use *slightly, a bit* or *a little* before a comparative to make the meaning weaker.
*This cottage is **slightly cheaper** than the other one.*

We can use *easily, by far* or *by a long way* before or after a superlative to make the meaning stronger.
*This is **easily / by far** the best trip I've been on.*
*This is the best trip I've been on **by far / by a long way**.*

so, such, too, enough

We use *too* + adjective / adverb to show that something is more than we want or need.
*It's **too cold** to go swimming.*
*She was speaking **too quickly** for me to understand.*

We use adjective / adverb + *enough*, or *enough* + noun to show something is or isn't as much as we want / need.
*The tent wasn't **big enough**.*
*I have **enough sandwiches** for everyone.*

Structures with *too* and *enough* are often followed by *to* + infinitive.
*That hotel is **too expensive to stay** in.*
*You need to be **strong enough to carry** all your own equipment.*

We use *so* and *such* for emphasis. It is stronger than *very*.
- We use *so* + adjective / adverb. *The sea was **so warm**!*
- We use *such* + (adjective) + noun. *This is **such an amazing view**.*

We can also use *so* and *such* with a *that* clause to emphasise characteristics that lead to a result or action.
*It was **such** an amazing view **that** I took 50 photos of it!*
*I was **so** tired **that** I fell asleep on the train.*

Grammar exercises

2 **Choose the correct option to complete the sentences.**

1 The journey wasn't as *smoother / smooth* as we had hoped it would be.
2 Antonio speaks English *less / the least* well than he used to.
3 Our flight to Madrid took *the longest / longer* than we expected.
4 The Empire State Building was once *the taller / the tallest* building in the world.
5 He didn't answer the questions as *quickly / quick* as I did.
6 This is *a bit / by far* the best food I've ever eaten.
7 The sea is warm *too / enough* to swim in.
8 The food is *too / enough* cold to eat.
9 It was *so / such* terrible weather that the streets were empty.
10 The sea was *so / such* rough that the boat trip was cancelled.

3 **Complete the sentences with the comparative or superlative form of the adjectives.**

1 Last night, I went to one of the _____ (good) concerts I have ever been to.
2 Living in the country is _____ (healthy) than living in a city.
3 Business Class is _____ (comfortable) than Economy.
4 Mount Everest is the _____ (high) mountain in the world.
5 This is _____ (delicious) food that I've ever eaten.
6 'How are you today?' 'Well, I feel _____ (bad) than yesterday.'

4 Rewrite the sentences with *as ... as* or *the* + comparative, *the* + comparative.

1 Flying to New York takes more time than flying to Athens.
Flying to Athens doesn't _____ .

2 You have visited more places in Scotland than I have.
I haven't _____ .

3 Shopping centres are more convenient than small shops.
Small shops aren't _____ .

4 James can run faster than Tim can.
Tim can't _____ .

5 You are more likely to have an accident when you drive fast.
The faster _____ .

6 If you work quickly, you'll be able to leave sooner.
The more quickly _____ .

7 As he went further into the forest, he became more frightened.
The further _____ .

8 As I learned more about the place, it seemed to be more interesting.
The more _____ .

5 Use the prompts to write comparative or superlative sentences.

1 I / run / much / fast / you
_____

2 Mo / drive / slightly / carefully / his brother
_____

3 The South Pole / be / by far / cold / place / the world
_____

4 This / be / easily / good / restaurant / the city
_____

5 Your hotel room / be / considerably / big / mine
_____

6 This / be / bad / journey / I / have / by a long way
_____

6 Write sentences with *too* or *enough*.

1 That car is very expensive. I can't buy it.
_____

2 Mike isn't tall. He can't be a firefighter.
_____

3 This coffee is very sweet. I can't drink it.
_____

4 Jake is very clever. He can solve the puzzle.
_____

7 Complete the sentences with one word in each gap.

1 My sister doesn't cook _____ well as I do. In other words, I am a much better cook _____ her.
2 Finn is _____ youngest boy in the class.
3 The smaller the rucksack you take, _____ easier it will be to carry.
4 She walks _____ slowly that people get impatient with her.
5 Yesterday was _____ a beautiful day.
6 I am not tall _____ to put my bag in that locker. Can you help, please?

Vocabulary

Phrasal verbs

8 Match the phrasal verbs (1–8) with their meanings (a–h).

1	book into	a	arrange for a room in a hotel
2	check in	b	exercise
3	check out	c	pay the bill and leave a hotel
4	head back	d	drive your car off the road and into a place
5	pull in	e	sleep at someone's house for a night
6	stay over	f	arrive and register at a hotel or airport
7	stop over	g	return
8	work out	h	stay at a place on the way to somewhere else

9 Complete the sentences with the correct form of the phrasal verbs from Exercise 8.

1 The driver needed a break, so we _____ to a roadside café for a drink.
2 The flight to Argentina isn't direct. We have to _____ in Madrid for three hours.
3 We always _____ a hotel close to the airport the night before we fly.
4 Ellen isn't at home tonight. She's _____ at her friend's house.
5 Danny is _____ in the hotel gym at the moment.
6 It's getting cold, so we're going to _____ now.
7 When we got to the airport, the first thing we did was _____ .
8 We _____ of the hotel at 1 a.m. and got a taxi to the station.

Prepositions

10 Choose the correct option to complete the sentences.

1 Uncle Jim is *in / on / within* a luxury cruise around the Bahamas at the moment.
2 Is there a doctor *in / on / within* board the ship?
3 We travelled south *in / on / within* search of sun, sea and sand.
4 Fortunately, there was a chemist *in / on / within* walking distance of our hotel.
5 Our team is *in / on / within* five points of winning the match.
6 I really hate having to stand *in / on / within* line at airports.

21

Collocations and expressions

11 Complete the sentences with these words.

compartment	crew	excess	gate	in-flight	pass

1 If you don't have a boarding _____ , they won't let you on the plane.

2 Please put your hand luggage in the overhead _____ .

3 I don't mind long plane journeys as long as there is plenty of _____ entertainment.

4 The cabin _____ on this plane are very friendly.

5 We bought so much on holiday that we had to pay for _____ baggage on the flight home.

6 Flight B34 to Berlin is ready for boarding at departure _____ 18.

Words easily confused

12 Complete the sentences with the correct form of these words. Use each word at least once.

1 | last | late | latest | latter | recent |
   |---|---|---|---|---|

   a She's the _____ person I expected to see here.

   b _____ research suggests that time travel might be possible.

   c Ben and Dan both showed great ability, but only the _____ won an Olympic medal.

   d His _____ film is set to become a blockbuster.

   e The _____ Dr Evans will be missed by family and friends alike.

2 | combine | join | share | stick |
   |---|---|---|---|

   a We had better _____ together, or we might get lost.

   b It's far from easy for me to _____ work with leisure.

   c Please _____ the water I gave you with your cousin.

   d How do I go about _____ the club?

3 | crossing | cruise | expedition | passage |
   |---|---|---|---|

   a Going on a world _____ sounds like fun.

   b Scott led a(n) _____ to the South Pole.

   c The _____ from the mainland to the island takes two hours.

   d Only the Red Cross workers were guaranteed safe _____ through the dangerous area.

4 | bank | border | boundary |
   |---|---|---|

   a We stayed in a small town near the Mexican _____ .

   b This wall marks the _____ between our property and theirs.

   c As a teenager, he spent hours fishing from the _____ of the river.

Word formation   suffixes

13 Use the word in capitals to form a word that fits in the gap.

1 _____ are responsible for most of the road accidents in this city.   **MOTOR**

2 Our flight from London was delayed, so we missed our _____ in Athens.   **CONNECT**

3 We took a shortcut through a _____ field.   **MUD**

4 It was windy at the airport, so we had a very bumpy _____ .   **LAND**

5 Any painting by Da Vinci is _____ – nobody could afford one.   **PRICE**

6 The journey was _____ longer than they expected.   **CONSIDER**

7 My mum is a medical _____ at City Hospital.   **CONSULT**

8 Our party will fight for liberty, freedom and _____ for all.   **EQUAL**

Sentence transformation

14 Complete the second sentence so that it has a similar meaning to the first sentence, using the word given. Do not change the word given. You must use between two and five words.

1 Felipe and Roberto are the same height.
TALL
Felipe _____ Roberto.

2 Sirius is the brightest star of all.
SHINES
Sirius _____ any other star.

3 She can't go away on holiday alone because she is too young.
OLD
She _____ to go away on holiday on her own.

4 This bed is so uncomfortable.
SUCH
This _____ bed.

5 Dubai is not nearly as far away as Tokyo.
MUCH
Tokyo is _____ Dubai.

6 We could walk from the hotel to the beach.
WITHIN
The beach _____ of our hotel.

7 When do we have to pay the bill and leave the hotel?
CHECK
What time do we have to _____ the hotel?

8 Do you exercise very often when you are on holiday?
WORK
How often _____ when you are on holiday?

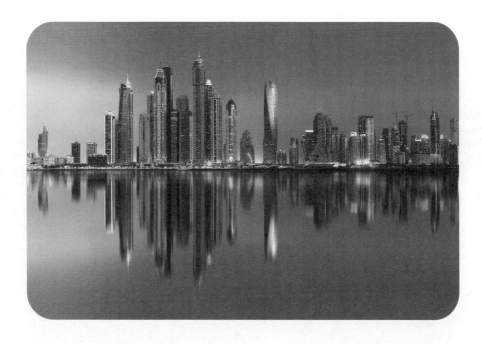

Awareness

1 Which of these sentences are correct (C) and incorrect (I)?

1 I'm a bit worried about missing the flight. ___
2 It was fairly freezing yesterday. ___
3 I am absolutely starving. ___
4 Andy was extremely annoyed. ___
5 It's very boiling in the sun today. ___

6 I got up lately because my alarm didn't go off. ___
7 Hurry up! You've hardly done anything so far. ___
8 The sea looks beautifully today. ___
9 Dan always seems very friendly. ___
10 I'm afraid your goldfish is extremely dead. ___

How many did you get right? ☐

Grammar

Gradable adjectives

Gradable adjectives can:
- vary in intensity.

It's **hot** today, but it was **very hot** yesterday.
- be used with grading adverbs such as *a little, extremely, fairly, hugely, immensely, intensely, rather, reasonably, slightly, unusually, very,* etc.

The hotel was **fairly big**, but it was **reasonably cheap**.
- have comparative and superlative forms.

The Science Museum was **more interesting** than the art exhibition, but the Cinema Museum was **the most interesting** of all.

Ungradable adjectives

Ungradable adjectives:
- cannot vary in intensity because they are already at their limit.

It was **boiling** in the middle of the day.
- are often used alone.

It was **freezing** in the mountains.
I was **furious** when my passport was stolen.
- can only be used with non-gradable adverbs such as *absolutely, utterly, completely, totally,* etc.

We were **completely exhausted** after travelling overnight.
That meal was **absolutely perfect**.

Note

The adverbs *really, fairly, pretty* and *quite* can often be used with gradable and non-gradable adjectives.
Jason is **pretty clever** for his age.
The book was **pretty terrible**, wasn't it?

Adjectives and adverbs

We usually form adverbs by adding -ly to an adjective.
helpful → helpful**ly**
quick → quick**ly**

If the adjective ends in -le, we change it to -ly.
gentle → gent**ly**
able → ab**ly**

If the adjective ends in -ic, we add -ally.
scientific → scientific**ally**
dramatic → dramatic**ally**

If the adjective already ends in -ly, we can't make an adverb, so we can use the structure in a / an … way.
lonely → **in a** lonely **way**
silly → **in a** silly **way**

Some words like hard, early, late, straight and fast can be both adjectives and adverbs.
Max is a **hard** worker. He works very **hard**.
We've got an **early** flight, so we need to get up **early**.
I wanted to watch the **late** film, so I went to bed very **late**.

The words hardly (= barely) and lately (= recently) are not the adverbs of hard and late.
Max **hardly** does any work. (= he does almost none)
Lately, I've been getting up very early. (= recently)

Verbs followed by adjectives

Most verbs can be followed by adverbs, to describe how they are done (e.g. drive slowly / carefully). However, a few verbs are followed by adjectives, which describe the subject, not the verb:

* be.
Lucy **is** friendly.

* verbs of 'becoming'.
Lucy **became** thirsty.
David **has gone** bald.
It's **getting** warm.
You're **growing** up.
His face **turned** pale.

* verbs of 'seeming'.
Lucy **seems** kind.
David **appears** confident.
The cake **looked** odd and it **smelled** unusual, but it **tasted** delicious.
You **sound** nervous.
It **feels** uncomfortable.

Grammar exercises

2 Choose the correct option to complete the sentences.

1 Elena was a bit *annoyed / furious* when her friend was late.
2 Are you absolutely *unsure / certain* that we don't need to book?
3 We had a very *excellent / good* taxi driver in Rio de Janeiro.
4 They were *completely / a little* exhausted after walking around the city all day.
5 The view from the top of the mountain was *utterly / slightly* beautiful.
6 The restaurant is *extremely / totally* popular, so we should book a table.

3 Complete the sentences with the adverb that best fits each gap.

1 That dessert was _____ good. (absolutely / very)

2 Luckily, the instructions were _____ easy to understand. (completely / fairly)

3 Tanya was _____ furious with Mario. (utterly / slightly)

4 The new restaurant turned out to be _____ excellent. (extremely / absolutely)

5 It's _____ impossible to find a room in Edinburgh at this time of the year. (virtually / very)

6 Are you totally _____ certain that Daniel hasn't been in today? (rather / totally)

7 We'd go outside, but it's _____ cold today. (totally / extremely)

8 The train fair to London is _____ cheap at weekends. (utterly / reasonably)

4 Complete the answers using these words.

| boiling | cold | freezing | hot | hungry | starving |

1 'What was the weather like?'

'It was absolutely _____ . We had to sit in the shade every lunchtime.'

2 'Shall I make you a sandwich?'

'Yes please – I'm completely _____ .'

3 'Would you like to go for a walk?'

'Not at the moment. It's quite _____ , and I don't have any gloves.'

4 'Are you OK? Your face is very red.'

'I'm fine, thanks – just a bit _____ because I've been running.'

5 'What would you like for lunch?'

'I'm not very _____ , so a sandwich will be fine.'

6 'Why are you wearing three jumpers?'

'Because it's utterly _____ in here!'

5 Choose the correct option to complete the sentences.

1 You look exhausted! Have you been working *hard / hardly*?

2 *Late / Lately*, I've started getting up half an hour earlier.

3 The tour guide introduced herself *friendly / in a friendly way* .

4 Do you think Alex is OK? He looks a bit *nervous / nervously*.

5 Luckily, there was *hard / hardly* any money in my purse when it was stolen.

6 I'm not going to eat this chicken sandwich. It doesn't smell *good / well*.

7 You should leave now if you don't want to arrive *late / lately*.

8 I don't want to watch that film. It sounds a bit *silly / in a silly way*.

Vocabulary

Phrasal verbs

6 **Match the phrasal verbs (1–8) with their meanings (a–h).**

1 let down ☐	a	go towards a place
2 make for ☐	b	say goodbye to someone at an airport, station, etc.
3 make out ☐	c	start a journey
4 run into ☐	d	arrive somewhere, sometimes unexpectedly
5 see off ☐	e	be able to see or hear something with difficulty
6 set off ☐	f	meet someone by chance
7 set up ☐	g	organise and establish something
8 turn up ☐	h	not do something that someone expects you to do

7 **Complete the sentences with the correct form of the phrasal verbs from Exercise 6.**

1 If you listen hard, you can just _____ the sound of music in the distance.

2 We _____ the twins at the airport yesterday.

3 When he finished university, he _____ his own software company.

4 She walked out of the hotel and _____ the beach.

5 We _____ in the city late at night with nowhere to stay.

6 What time shall we _____ for the station tomorrow?

7 I wasn't happy when my friend _____ me _____ .

8 I couldn't believe it when I _____ an old friend at the bus stop in Milan.

Prepositions

8 **Choose the correct option to complete the sentences.**

1 We were *at / by / with* sea for four weeks, and I was getting tired of it.

2 Two thousand miles is a long way to travel *at / by / with* car.

3 I think there's something wrong *at / by / with* you if you don't like going to the beach.

4 That was *at / by / with* far the best meal we have had so far this holiday.

5 He was stopped by the police driving down the motorway *at / by / with* 120 miles per hour.

6 I went into hospital *at / by / with* food poisoning on the first day of the holiday.

Collocations and expressions

9 **Complete the sentences with the correct form of these words.**

get	give	have	hold	put	take

1 I'd love to _____ a trip to Australia and New Zealand.

2 The government has _____ limits on the number of climbers allowed on the mountain.

3 What do you think the future _____ for eco-tourism?

4 Can you _____ me an idea of how many nights you'd like to stay in each place?

5 Buenos Aires and Madrid _____ a lot of things in common.

6 Sorry we're late – we _____ stuck in some very slow traffic.

22

Words easily confused

10 Complete the sentences with the correct form of these words. Use each word at least once.

1 know   realise   recognise   understand

   a Although I hadn't been there for 30 years, I _____ the house immediately.

   b I don't _____ what this street is called.

   c It wasn't until we arrived that I _____ I'd been there before.

   d In order to _____ the map, you need to be able to interpret the symbols.

2 damp   humid   mild   wet

   a Where have you been? You're _____ through!

   b We'd been expecting lots of snow but it turned out to be a _____ winter.

   c Having lived in the tropics, he's used to a _____ climate.

   d The old cottage is _____ inside because it has been empty for a year.

3 alive   live   lively   living

   a My oldest _____ relative is 88 years old.

   b The match will be shown _____ at ten o'clock.

   c When the rescue team found her, she was still _____ .

   d Having _____ children around the house is exhausting but fun.

4 pollute   rot   spoil   stain

   a They _____ the whole evening by insulting everyone they spoke to.

   b I'm afraid the drink you spilled has _____ the carpet.

   c As the wooden window frames had _____ , we replaced them.

   d If we go on _____ the rivers, all living things in them will die.

Word formation   mixed

11 Use the word in capitals to form a word that fits in the gap.

   1 Please be careful when driving on _____ roads.   **ICE**

   2 My travel guides are arranged _____ .   **ALPHABET**

   3 His ambition is to have a successful career in _____ .   **JOURNAL**

   4 What a strange _____   **COINCIDE**

   5 We had a(n) _____ wet April this year – in fact, it was the wettest on record.   **USUAL**

   6 I think it is _____ to tell lies to children, so I never do it.   **MORAL**

   7 We had to _____ the entire first scene because the director didn't like the first version.   **WRITE**

   8 She stared at her _____ in the mirror.   **REFLECT**

Sentence transformation

12 Complete the second sentence so that it has a similar meaning to the first sentence, using the word given. Do not change the word given. You must use between two and five words.

1 After walking in the mountains all day, we were extremely tired.
   COMPLETELY
   After walking in the mountains all day _____ .

2 Eva wasn't just a little bit annoyed with Mark.
   ABSOLUTELY
   Eva was _____ with Mark.

3 Sophie is a very fast runner.
   EXTREMELY
   Sophie runs _____ .

4 When I first saw the man, I thought I knew him.
   FAMILIAR
   When I first saw the man, he _____ .

5 Sanjay had been waiting nearly half an hour when Priya finally arrived.
   UP
   Sanjay had been waiting nearly half an hour when Priya finally _____ .

6 Let's head in the direction of the hills.
   MAKE
   Let's _____ the hills.

7 I'd love to visit Southern Asia one day.
   TAKE
   I'd love to _____ Southern Asia one day.

8 They started the eco-travel company in 2015.
   SET
   They _____ the eco-travel company in 2015.

Awareness

1 Which of these sentences are correct (C) and incorrect (I)?

1 I wish I know how to speak Arabic. ___
2 If only you hadn't lost your address book. ___
3 Are you OK? You look as you need to lie down. ___
4 It's about time I went home. ___
5 I'd much rather to stay at home tonight. ___

6 Would you prefer to live in the country? ___
7 I rather eat an apple than a banana. ___
8 I wish I could fly. ___
9 She prefers junk food. ___
10 If only you weren't so stubborn. ___

How many did you get right? [ ]

Grammar

Wishes

We use *wish* to talk about a situation or an action we are not happy about, or to say how we would like something to be different. We use *wish* + past simple or continuous when we talk about the present or the future.
I wish I knew how to do karate.
I wish I were playing football this weekend.

We use *wish* + past perfect simple or continuous when we talk about the past.
I wish I hadn't slept for so long this morning.
I wish I'd been listening when the coach explained the rules.

We use *wish* + *would* + infinitive when we talk about other people's annoying habits or to say that we would like something to be different in the future. We use it for actions, not states. Do not use *wish* + *would* when the subjects are the same; use *wish* + *could* + infinitive instead.
I wish the school canteen would sell more fruit.
I wish the gym would stop putting up their prices every year.
I wish I could run more than once a week. (not: I wish I would ...)

We can use *If only* instead of *wish* in affirmative and negative sentences when we feel especially strongly about something.
If only I didn't have a broken arm.
If only I hadn't lost my tennis racket.

as if and as though

We can use *as if* and *as though* to say what something is similar to. There is no difference in meaning between *as if* and *as though*. They are usually followed by 'normal' tenses (i.e. present to talk about the present; past to talk about the past), whether we're talking about something real / likely or unreal / unlikely.
Are you OK? You sound as if you're tired.
After running 10 km, I felt as though I was running through thick mud.

When we are talking about the unreal present, we can choose whether to use the present or the past. Both forms are equally good and mean the same.
It's too early for me – it's as if I'm / I were still asleep.

it's (about / high) time ...

We can use *it's time*, *it's about time* and *it's high time* + past tense to talk about something that should have already been done in the present.
It's time you started doing more regular exercise.
It's about time I went to the dentist's.
It's high time Tim stopped eating junk food.

would rather

We use *would rather* to show a preference in the present or future. We use *would rather* + infinitive when we are talking about ourselves.
I'd rather run outside than in a gym.

We use *would rather* followed by a pronoun and a past tense when we are talking about someone else in the present or future.
I'd rather we went to a restaurant than cooked at home this evening.

would prefer and prefer

We use *would prefer* to show preference in a particular situation (not in general). We can use:
- *would prefer + noun.*
'Would you like salad or chips with that?'
'I'd prefer salad.'
- *would prefer + to + infinitive.*
I'd prefer to stay in tonight.
- *would prefer + to + infinitive + rather than + infinitive.*
I'd prefer to go swimming rather than go to the gym.

We use prefer to show preference in general. We can use:
- *prefer + noun.*
I prefer fruit juice (to fizzy drinks).
- *prefer + to + infinitive + rather than + infinitive.*
I prefer to eat potatoes rather than eat chips.
- *prefer + -ing + to + -ing.*
I prefer doing sport to watching sport.

Grammar exercises

2 Choose the correct option to complete the sentences.

1 Maria wishes she *can / could* type faster.
2 I wish I *spoke / speak* French.
3 She wishes she *learned / had learned* Spanish when she was much younger.
4 I have put on a lot of weight. If only I *didn't eat / hadn't eaten* so much on holiday.
5 If only I *could go / went* on holiday next month.
6 I wish I *bought / had bought* that car a year ago.
7 James wishes he *didn't sleep / hadn't slept* on the beach. Now he's sunburned.
8 I wish Mary *doesn't drive / didn't drive* so fast.
9 They wish I *came / had come* home earlier last night.
10 If only I *could come / came* with you tomorrow.

3 Complete the sentences with one word in each gap.

1 I _____ I knew how to dance.
2 If _____ I had tried this years ago.
3 He looks as _____ he needs some water.
4 It's about _____ you learned how to cook.
5 I'd _____ cook pasta than boil rice.
6 I prefer to relax at home rather _____ do tiring sports.

23

4 Complete the sentences with *prefer* or *rather*.

1 Do you _____ swimming in a pool or in the sea?
2 I'd _____ a smaller portion, please. I'm not very hungry.
3 I'd _____ we went to the rugby match than the football match.
4 You'd _____ play basketball than volleyball, wouldn't you?
5 Would you _____ to play tennis tomorrow or on Thursday?
6 To be honest, I'd _____ not play with you if you are going to cheat.

5 Complete the sentences with the correct form of the verbs.

1 If only I _____ (have) more money. I'd like to buy that surfboard.
2 She wishes she _____ (study) medicine when she had the chance.
3 My father loves sailing. He wishes he _____ (live) nearer the sea.
4 I wish I _____ (study). I can't concentrate.
5 I wish you _____ (come) to yoga classes with me.
6 Amelie wishes I _____ (not / tell) everybody about the party.
7 Jack wishes he _____ (not / eat) so much. Now he feels awful.
8 If only our neighbours _____ (turn) the volume down a little. I can't sleep.

6 Complete the sentences with these verbs and *It's time*.

buy	cut	go	grow	have	wash

1 'My car is very dirty.'
  ' *It's time you washed* _____ it.'
2 'The grass is really long in our garden.'
  '_____ it.'
3 'My computer is eight years old.'
  '_____ a new one.'
4 'I've been working too hard recently.'
  '_____ on holiday.'
5 'My hair is too long.'
  '_____ it cut.'
6 'John is acting like a child.'
  '_____ up.'

7 Correct the sentences where necessary. Tick those which do not need correcting.

1 I'd prefer eat in tonight.

   _____

2 Do you prefer swimming or surfing?

   _____

3 I prefer healthy food than fast food.

   _____

4 He'd prefer to sleep in a tent rather sleep on a sofa.

   _____

5 I prefer dancing to sing.

   _____

6 Would you prefer to go alone?

   _____

Vocabulary

Phrasal verbs

8 Match the phrasal verbs (1–8) with their meanings (a–h).

1	bring up	☐	**a**	get an illness
2	care for	☐	**b**	vomit
3	clear up	☐	**c**	become conscious again
4	come down with	☐	**d**	begin to talk about a particular subject
5	come round	☐	**e**	(of a vehicle) stop by the roadside temporarily
6	pull up	☐	**f**	look after someone who is sick or can't look after themselves
7	stand up for	☐	**g**	make tidy
8	throw up	☐	**h**	defend something or somebody from attack

9 Complete the sentences with the correct form of the phrasal verbs from Exercise 8.

1 I didn't feel well on the boat because the sea was rough. I almost _____ .

2 A car _____ next to me while I was waiting for a bus – it was my uncle.

3 Don't forget to _____ the subject of the lunch menu at the next meeting.

4 I _____ the flu on the first day of the summer holidays.

5 When he _____ , he was lying on the pavement surrounded by people.

6 His big sister always _____ him in the playground, so he never got bullied.

7 Can you _____ this mess before I cook dinner, please?

8 I was very grateful to the nurses who _____ me in hospital.

Prepositions

10 Choose the correct option to complete the sentences.

1 By the time I saw the dentist I was *in / under / up* agony.

2 You ought to take up a sport, because you are *in / under / up* really bad shape at the moment.

3 After three weeks in bed, my grandmother was finally *in / under / up* and about.

4 If you're feeling *in / under / up* the weather, why not take the day off?

5 Children are *in / under / up* a lot of pressure to succeed at school these days.

6 Someone was riding a motorbike *in / under / up* and down the street late last night.

Collocations and expressions

11 Complete the sentences with the correct form of these verbs.

apply   catch   hold   lose   skip   take

1 If you _____ a cold, you should rest and drink lots of water.

2 Take this cream and _____ it to your cut.

3 I was late, so I _____ breakfast and went straight to school.

4 Lie down and I'll _____ your temperature.

5 How long can you _____ your breath under water?

6 Nick can't give his presentation today – he has _____ his voice.

23

Words easily confused

12 Complete the sentences with the correct form of these words. Use each word at least once.

1 contest   event   game   match

   a I'm not in the mood for a(n) _____ of cards.

   b After winning a talent _____ , she appeared on national television.

   c The charity cricket match is the village's most popular annual _____ .

   d Several football _____ had to be postponed due to heavy snow.

2 crest   lid   peak   top

   a There was a crow's nest at the _____ of the tree.

   b The surfer stayed on the _____ of a wave for a few seconds before falling into the water.

   c At the _____ of her career, she earned vast sums of money.

   d He couldn't get the _____ off the biscuit tin.

3 direct   immediate   instant   straight

   a There are no _____ flights to Washington from this airport.

   b She was so tired that she went _____ to bed.

   c The residents cut off by the floods are in no _____ danger.

   d I haven't got enough _____ coffee to make us all a cup.

4 chop   grate   peel   slice

   a Could you _____ some cheese to put on the spaghetti, please?

   b I can never _____ a potato without wasting half of it.

   c _____ the parsley on this board, will you?

   d They'll _____ the ham for you at the supermarket.

Word formation   noun → adjective

13 Use the word in capitals to form a word that fits in the gap.

   1 You look _____ in that pirate costume.   **RIDICULE**

   2 We cycle more than we drive because it is more _____ .   **ECOLOGY**

   3 That film has a very _____ ending.   **DRAMA**

   4 I have never had such a _____ toothache in my life!   **PAIN**

   5 We found a _____ old bike at the bottom of the garden.   **RUST**

   6 He didn't expect his business to be very _____ , but it was.   **PROFIT**

   7 It is not a good idea to set up a factory in a _____ area.   **RESIDENT**

   8 You don't have to study a language here – it's _____ .   **OPTION**

Sentence transformation

14 Complete the second sentence so that it has a similar meaning to the first sentence, using the word given. Do not change the word given. You must use between two and five words.

1 Your bedroom really needs to be painted.

HIGH

It's _____ was painted.

2 I'm not going to the beach this weekend, but I would like to.

WAS

I wish _____ the beach this weekend.

3 Going to the park would be better than doing homework.

RATHER

I _____ to the park than do homework.

4 Sue thinks it's better to ride than to walk.

PREFERS

Sue _____ walking.

5 Greg is always protected by his best friend.

STANDS

Greg's best friend _____ him.

6 I caught a cold on my first day of school.

DOWN

I _____ on my first day of school.

7 Mum is finally able to get out of bed again.

ABOUT

Mum is finally _____ again.

8 You are always tired because of your poor physical condition.

SHAPE

You are _____ , which is why you are always tired.

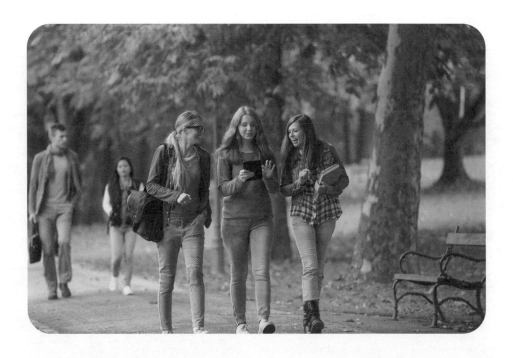

Awareness

1 **Which of these sentences are correct (C) and incorrect (I)?**

1 Not only did he win, but he also broke the record. ___
2 Never she had seen such a boring film. ___
3 Under no circumstances are you allowed in here. ___
4 Seldom you see a bear in a suit. ___
5 Not once anyone came to help me. ___

6 Little did he know the police were waiting for him. ___
7 No sooner we had got home than the electricity went off. ___
8 Only then did he realise his mistake. ___
9 Not since I was a child I've ridden a horse. ___
10 Rarely does she swim in the sea. ___

How many did you get right? ☐

Grammar

Negative inversion

We can use certain negative words and expressions at the beginning of a sentence for emphasis. When we do this, the word order changes. The auxiliary verb comes before the subject. This is called inversion. If there is no auxiliary verb (i.e. we are using the present or past simple), we use *do / does / did*, in exactly the same way as when we're making questions.

I've never seen such a beautiful forest.
Never have I seen such a beautiful forest!

Jake not only fixes computers, he makes them.
Not only does Jake *fix* computers, but he also makes them.

You are not allowed to take photos here *under any circumstances*.
Under no circumstances are you allowed to take photos here.

We had no idea that the restaurant would be so busy.
Little did we know that the restaurant would be so busy.

You rarely / seldom see children playing outside.
Rarely / Seldom do you see children playing outside.

The instructor didn't help me once with the routine.
Not once did the instructor help me with the routine.

I didn't realise I'd left my goggles at the pool before I got home.
I got home. *Only then did I realise* that I'd left my goggles at the pool.

It started to rain when we got into the boat.
No sooner / Hardly had we got into the boat when it started to rain.

I haven't done gymnastics *since* I was at school.
Not since I was at school *have I done* gymnastics.

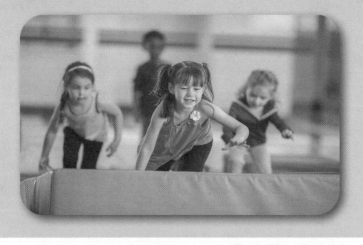

Grammar exercises

2 Choose the correct option to complete the sentences.

1 Little *they knew / did they know* that it would rain all day.
2 Rarely do *I have / have I* eggs for breakfast.
3 Under no circumstances *are children / children are* allowed here without an adult.
4 Never *she had / had she* run so quickly.
5 Not since *they were / were they* on holiday had they been surfing.
6 Hardly *they had / had they* started cooking when the guests arrived.
7 Only then *he realised / did he realise* he hadn't brought his wallet.
8 Not once *did I manage / I managed* to hit the ball over the net.
9 Not only *she plays / does she play* basketball, she's also a fast runner.
10 Seldom *does he go / he goes* into the office these days.

3 Write sentences with Not only ... , but also ... .

1 They spent a month in Bali. They also spent a month in the Bahamas.

_____

2 She owns a large flat in the city. She has a villa in the country, too.

_____

3 She had been spying on the diplomat. She had also given him false information.

_____

4 The car is very fast. It is safe, too.

_____

5 It was very cold. There was also a strong wind.

_____

6 He's a great guitarist. He's a brilliant songwriter, too.

_____

4 Choose the correct beginning (a–c) to complete the sentences.

1 ___ has Barry won a race.
   a Never   **b** Little   **c** Not only

2 ___ had we sat down to eat than the baby started to cry.
   a Only then   **b** Hardly   **c** Had

3 ___ are dogs allowed in the shop.
   a No sooner   **b** Little   **c** Under no circumstances

4 ___ did I know they had made me a birthday cake.
   a Not only   **b** Little   **c** No sooner

5 ___ he been informed, he would have acted differently.
   a Seldom   **b** Only   **c** Had

6 ___ did anyone ask why I was there.
   a Not only   **b** Not once   **c** Little

5 **Rewrite the sentences using inversion.**

1 I have never had such a great time.

Never _____ .

2 You may not, under any circumstances, leave the room while the exam is in progress.

Under no _____ .

3 She had no idea that there was a surprise party waiting for her when she got home.

Little _____ .

4 You rarely see a police officer on a bicycle these days.

Rarely _____ .

5 She did not stop once for a rest.

Not once _____ .

6 As soon as I shut the door, I realised my keys were still inside.

No sooner _____ .

7 If she had remembered her umbrella, she would have stayed dry.

Had _____ .

6 **Complete the sentences with one word in each gap.**

1 _____ no circumstances is anyone allowed into this room.

2 Not _____ does he play football, but he also plays tennis.

3 Little _____ we know that our tour guide was actually a professor.

4 Only _____ did I realise I'd forgotten my swimming costume.

5 _____ you asked for permission first, nobody would have objected.

6 No _____ had they unpacked the picnic than it started to rain.

Vocabulary

Phrasal verbs

7 **Match the phrasal verbs (1–8) with their meanings (a–h).**

1 burn out ☐
2 cut off ☐
3 fight off ☐
4 get over ☐
5 pass on ☐
6 pass out ☐
7 take away ☐
8 wear off ☐

8 **Complete the sentences with the correct form of the phrasal verbs from Exercise 7.**

1 The flood waters rose so high that our whole village was _____ from the surrounding villages.

2 When you tell Maria the news, you can be sure she'll _____ it _____ !

3 It took a few months for Ben to _____ his broken leg.

4 It was so hot that day that many of the spectators _____ and had to be taken to hospital.

5 You need to take some time off soon, or you might _____ .

6 There are many different drugs you can take to _____ the flu these days.

7 As the effects of the painkillers _____ , I became more and more uncomfortable.

8 My parents _____ my tablet as punishment for failing all of my exams.

Prepositions

9 **Choose the correct option to complete the sentences.**

1 Are you allergic *for* / *from* / *to* dairy products?
2 Perhaps he will benefit *of* / *from* / *to* a course of vitamin tablets.
3 If you have had all your vaccinations, you should be immune *for* / *from* / *to* all the major childhood diseases.
4 It didn't take long for Rosie to get sick *of* / *from* / *to* the hospital food.
5 Fortunately, I don't suffer *for* / *from* / *to* any allergies.
6 A lack *of* / *from* / *to* vitamin C is one reason why your teeth bleed when you brush them.

Collocations and expressions

10 **Complete the sentences with these words.**

birth   breath   good   shape   stomach   what

1 I try to keep in _____ by cycling to work and running twice a week.
2 Do you think a walk in the forest would do you _____ ?
3 Kate has an upset _____ , so she doesn't feel like eating.
4 Alex is out of _____ because he's just been running.
5 Laura gave _____ to a baby boy at four o'clock this morning.
6 As the saying goes: you are _____ you eat!

Words easily confused

11 **Complete the sentences with the correct form of these words. Use each word at least once.**

1 | base   bed   bottom   end |
|---|

   a Apparently, there is a lot of treasure lying on the sea _____ .
   b There must be several unknown species living at the _____ of the ocean.
   c The statue stands on a marble _____ .
   d Many people have predicted the _____ of the world.

2 | cure   heal   recover   treat |
|---|

   a He was taken to Walton Hospital, where he was _____ for shock.
   b It'll take time for her to _____ from her injuries.
   c The wound _____ more quickly than I anticipated.
   d If this stuff doesn't _____ you, I don't know what will.

3 | close   draw   shut   turn off |
|---|

   a Talks are going smoothly and we hope to _____ the deal this evening.
   b _____ the radio for a moment.
   c Please _____ the door on the way out.
   d When it gets dark, _____ the curtains.

4 | complete   total   whole |
|---|

   a It took three _____ weeks to repair the robot.
   b They won't stop until the work is _____ .
   c The _____ number of students present is 91.
   d I'll give you £50 for the _____ lot.
   e These volumes contain the _____ works of Shakespeare.
   f You must tell the _____ truth.

Word formation   mixed

12 Complete the sentences with a form of the word in capitals

1 What a _____ dress you're wearing tonight!   COLOUR

2 Anna's _____ has never prevented her doing the things she really   DISABLE
  wants to do.

3 The children complained _____ throughout the entire car journey.   CONTINUE

4 Tragically, there were no _____ of the accident.   SURVIVE

5 I couldn't get rid of the horrible feeling of _____ I had since I'd woken up.   SICK

6 Germs enter your blood _____ , and that is how you catch the disease.   VISIBLE

7 Some people have a dangerous _____ to nuts.   REACT

8 He is an imaginative child, but he sometimes has difficulty in distinguishing
  _____ from fantasy.   REAL

Sentence transformation

13 Complete the second sentence so that it has a similar meaning to the first sentence, using the word
given. Do not change the word given. You must use between two and five words.

1 It only hurts when I laugh.
  DOES
  Only _____ hurt.

2 You seldom see three-wheeled cars these days.
  DO
  Seldom _____ three-wheeled cars these days.

3 Animals are never allowed in the hotel rooms.
  CIRCUMSTANCES
  Under _____ allowed in the hotel rooms.

4 As soon as we switched off the lights, the music started.
  SOONER
  No _____ the lights than the music started.

5 He's an excellent cook, and he eats really healthily.
  ONLY
  Not _____ an excellent cook, he also eats really healthily.

6 It was so hot in the stadium that I thought I would become unconscious.
  OUT
  It was so hot in the stadium that I thought I _____ .

7 As time passes, the effects of the drug will become weaker.
  WEAR
  The effects of the drug _____ as time passes.

8 These pills will do you good.
  BENEFIT
  You _____ these pills.

B2 Practice: First

Part 1

For questions 1–8, read the text below and decide which answer (A, B, C or D) best fits each gap. There is an example at the beginning (0).

Modern tourism

Tourism has **(0)** ___ in for a lot of criticism recently. One common fault found with it is that **(1)** ___ no longer broadens the mind. But why should it? Surely, the holidaymakers who choose to go on a package tour know just what such a holiday **(2)** ___ . This is what **(3)** ___ to them, so why shouldn't they go on this type of holiday? Travel writers generally **(4)** ___ down on them because of their lack of adventure – 'all they want is a room with a sea view!' But what if they don't want broader minds? Maybe they choose these holiday **(5)** ___ because their minds can't get any broader!

Another criticism levelled at tourism concerns the changes **(6)** ___ at holiday destinations: the local culture changes, land is developed and **(7)** ___ roads are built. The tourist is provided with a copy of the place he or she has just left, plus service. So why should there be any criticism? The world is changing rapidly and neither you nor I have the **(8)** ___ to stop it. Or do we … ?

0	(A) come	B	gone	C	stayed	D	been
1	A journey	B	voyage	C	travel	D	expedition
2	A involves	B	forms	C	consists	D	holds
3	A draws	B	pleases	C	attracts	D	appeals
4	A see	B	look	C	let	D	keep
5	A resorts	B	ports	C	places	D	shores
6	A watched	B	viewed	C	observed	D	glanced
7	A principal	B	significant	C	main	D	chief
8	A ability	B	qualification	C	skill	D	talent

Part 2

For questions 9–16, read the text below and think of the word which best fits each gap. Use only one word in each gap. There is an example at the beginning (0).

The other point of view

Very often a disagreement (0) __between__ two friends, neighbours or colleagues can lead to problems. In order to avoid falling (9) _____ with a friend, neighbour or workmate, it is always an excellent idea to try to see the other person's point of view. If you carefully consider how (10) _____ else thinks, your own thinking might improve, so write down the views your friend, neighbour or colleague is likely to have. Not only will their thoughts surprise you, but you may (11) _____ find a solution to the problem.

Recently a friend of mine bought a new printer. The dealer in the shop had recommended it, but she was let (12) _____ when she found out it was no better than her old one. Before taking it back, she had a thought. She realised that if the dealer was criticised, he (13) _____ be offended. So, instead of complaining, she said that she had (14) _____ a mistake by not asking for the right printer. The dealer changed it free of charge. If my friend (15) _____ not handled the problem in this way, the dealer would not have provided her (16) _____ a free replacement.

Part 3

For questions 17–24, read the text below. Use the word given in capitals at the end of some of the lines to form a word that fits in the gap in the same line. There is an example at the beginning (0).

A stressful time

Life is stressful for all of us sometimes. However, most of us would agree that the most

(0) _____confusing_____ time in a person's life is adolescence. It is a time when **CONFUSE**

(17) _____ that will affect a person's future have to be made. Perhaps this is **CHOOSE**

unfortunate, because it is also the time when teenagers are so distracted by other things that they

may not be capable of making such decisions. (18) _____ comes at a time when **DEPEND**

it is most difficult to handle.

These two factors, together with the pressure to be academically (19) _____ , can **SUCCESS**

mean that sometimes teenagers behave badly when they are subject to (20) _____ . **CRITIC**

All too often adults regard those in their teens as being (21) _____ , and make **THINK**

continuous (22) _____ about their attitude towards older people. Yet, if an adult **COMPLAIN**

under stress behaves unnaturally at any time, things are different. (23) _____ from **RUDE**

an adult, for example, may be excused because they are under pressure. Why is this? People tend

to lose (24) _____ of the fact that adolescents are also under great pressure when **SEE**

going through this difficult time of their lives.

Part 4

For questions 25–30, complete the second sentence so that it has a similar meaning to the first sentence, using the word given. Do not change the word given. You must use between two and five words, including the word given. Here is an example (0).

Example:

0 Adam plays hockey. He is also a great dancer.
   ONLY
   Not _____ *only does Adam play hockey* _____ , he's also a great dancer.

25 Many people think that scientists have received signals from other life forms.
    THOUGHT
    Scientists _____ signals from other life forms.

26 Taking care of four young children is difficult.
    LOOK
    It isn't _____ four young children.

27 We enjoyed ourselves at the beach.
    TIME
    We _____ at the beach.

28 What they need to do is form a new committee.
    OUGHT
    They really _____ up a new committee.

29 Be very quiet and you can watch me repair the clock.
    LONG
    You can watch me repair the clock _____ very quiet.

30 He drew cartoons before he began making films.
    WORKED
    He _____ before he began making films.

B2 Practice: ECCE

Grammar

For questions 1–20, choose the word or phrase that best completes the sentence or conversation.

1 I'm not as sporty ___ you.
   A   as
   B   like
   C   than
   D   for

2 The hotter the weather, the ___ it is at the beach.
   A   busy
   B   busier
   C   busiest
   D   busily

3 Never ___ such a friendly person.
   A   I've met
   B   have I met
   C   I'm meeting
   D   am I meeting

4 If only he ___ about the new rules.
   A   knows
   B   is knowing
   C   had known
   D   have known

5 The further he ran, the ___ he became.
   A   more tired
   B   tireder
   C   most tired
   D   tiredest

6 I'm not ___ to join the club, it's just for adults.
   A   enough old
   B   too old
   C   old enough
   D   old too

7 I'm sorry, you're ___ to watch this film.
   A   young enough
   B   enough young
   C   young too
   D   too young

8 That photograph is ___ beautiful.
   A   such
   B   so
   C   enough
   D   much

9 The film was ___ good.
   A   absolutely
   B   totally
   C   utterly
   D   extremely

10 I need some fresh air – it's ___ boiling in here!
   A   a little
   B   fairly
   C   hugely
   D   absolutely

11 Rarely ___ abroad on holiday.
   A   we do go
   B   go we
   C   do we go
   D   we go

12 He's the ___ man I know.
   A   braver
   B   bravest
   C   most brave
   D   more brave

13 It's ___ time you learned to swim!
   A   high
   B   low
   C   tall
   D   around

14 I prefer ___ rather than take public transport.
   A   driving
   B   drive
   C   driven
   D   to drive

15 That was ___ ride ever!
   A   the excitingest
   B   the more exciting
   C   the exciting
   D   the most exciting

16 ___ there been such a celebration in this house!
   A   There never
   B   Has ever
   C   Never has
   D   Has never

17 'Shall we go out?'
   ' ___ stay in.'
   A   I'd rather
   B   I've rather
   C   I'm rather
   D   I'll rather

18 You're ___ baby!
   A   such a
   B   so
   C   such
   D   so a

19 Not ___ do they misbehave, but they won't eat!
   A   just
   B   solely
   C   alone
   D   only

20 We arrived later ___ anyone.
   A   as
   B   like
   C   than
   D   for

Vocabulary

For questions 21–40, choose the word or phrase that most appropriately completes the sentence.

21 I like to ___ out in the gym three times a week.
A check
B work
C pull
D figure

22 You shouldn't ___ breakfast – it's important.
A jump
B skip
C leap
D hop

23 What time do we have to check ___ when we leave?
A up
B down
C in
D out

24 Why do we always have to stand in ___ for ages in this place?
A line
B queue
C row
D wait

25 Rosie always stands ___ for her sister at school.
A in
B out
C up
D down

26 I'm already sick ___ boiled eggs for breakfast.
A from
B to
C of
D about

27 She's exhausted – she's just ___ birth.
A given
B taken
C kept
D had

28 I've had a(n) ___ stomach, so I'll just have toast.
A anxious
B sad
C tired
D upset

29 When the sun came out, they made ___ the beach.
A out
B for
C off
D away

30 I couldn't ___ what the words said.
A make out
B make off
C make up
D make over

31 How long were you ___ sea for?
A on
B in
C by
D at

32 She passed ___ in fright at the sight of the shark.
A out
B off
C under
D up

33 He ___ up this company at the age of 20.
A made
B did
C put
D set

34 I hope you've booked us ___ a nice hotel.
A up
B into
C over
D in

35 When did you come ___ with this cold?
A down
B up
C over
D across

36 It's a long way to walk, but it's ___ cycling distance.
A in
B with
C within
D on

37 Oh no! We've ___ stuck behind a tractor!
A given
B got
C put
D taken

38 Call a doctor. I'm ___ agony!
A under
B with
C in
D on

39 Dan will call you later – he's ___ his voice!
A lost
B missed
C held
D taken

40 I'm trying to ___ off the flu at the moment, but I'm not succeeding.
A push
B battle
C box
D fight

Irregular verbs

Infinitive	Past simple	Past participle
be	was / were	been
beat	beat	beaten
become	became	become
begin	began	begun
bite	bit	bitten
blow	blew	blown
break	broke	broken
bring	brought	brought
broadcast	broadcast	broadcast
build	built	built
burn	burned / burnt	burned / burnt
buy	bought	bought
can	could	–
catch	caught	caught
choose	chose	chosen
come	came	come
cost	cost	cost
cut	cut	cut
deal	dealt	dealt
do	did	done
draw	drew	drawn
dream	dreamed / dreamt	dreamed / dreamt
drink	drank	drunk
drive	drove	driven
eat	ate	eaten
fall	fell	fallen
feed	fed	fed
feel	felt	felt
fight	fought	fought
find	found	found
fly	flew	flown
forbid	forbade	forbidden
forget	forgot	forgotten
freeze	froze	frozen
get	got	got
give	gave	given
go	went	gone
grow	grew	grown
hang	hung	hung
have	had	had
hear	heard	heard
hide	hid	hidden
hit	hit	hit
hold	held	held
hurt	hurt	hurt
keep	kept	kept
know	knew	known
learn	learned / learnt	learned / learnt
leave	left	left
lend	lent	lent
let	let	let

Infinitive	Past simple	Past participle
lie	lay	lain
light	lit	lit
lose	lost	lost
make	made	made
mean	meant	meant
meet	met	met
mow	mowed	mowed / mown
pay	paid	paid
prove	proved	proven
put	put	put
read	read (pronounced /red/)	read (pronounced /red/)
ride	rode	ridden
ring	rang	rung
run	ran	run
say	said	said
see	saw	seen
sell	sold	sold
send	sent	sent
set	set	set
shake	shook	shaken
shine	shone	shone
shoot	shot	shot
show	showed	shown
shut	shut	shut
sing	sang	sung
sit	sat	sat
sleep	slept	slept
slide	slid	slid
smell	smelt	smelt
speak	spoke	spoken
spend	spent	spent
spoil	spoiled / spoilt	spoiled / spoilt
spread	spread	spread
stand	stood	stood
steal	stole	stolen
stick	stuck	stuck
stink	stank	stunk
swim	swam	swum
take	took	taken
teach	taught	taught
tear	tore	torn
tell	told	told
think	thought	thought
throw	threw	thrown
understand	understood	understood
wake	woke	woken
wear	wore	worn
win	won	won
write	wrote	written

Phrasal verbs

act as	=	do a job for a short time	(U17)
add to	=	increase the size, number or amount of something	(U15)
back up	=	make a spare copy of something on a computer	(U9)
be taken in	=	be fooled or cheated by someone	(U10)
believe in	=	be sure that something is right	(U12)
block out	=	stop light or noise passing through	(U15)
blow over	=	(of a storm or argument) end without causing harm	(U15)
blow up	=	destroy with a bomb	(U15)
book into	=	arrange for a room in a hotel	(U21)
bottle up	=	hide strong emotions	(U2)
break down	=	suddenly stop working	(U9)
breeze through	=	succeed easily	(U19)
bring up	=	begin to talk about a particular subject	(U23)
burn down	=	destroy something (usually a building) with fire	(U13)
burn out	=	become too ill or tired to do any more work	(U2), (U24)
burst out	=	begin doing something suddenly	(U12)
call (sb) back	=	telephone somebody again	(U3)
call for	=	require or demand	(U4)
call off	=	cancel an event	(U3)
call on	=	ask	(U4)
call round	=	visit somebody's house	(U3)
calm down	=	become less excited	(U2)
care for	=	look after someone who is sick or can't look after themselves	(U23)
catch on	=	become popular	(U5)
catch up on	=	find out what's been happening	(U5)
check in	=	arrive and register at a hotel or airport	(U21)
check out	=	pay the bill and leave a hotel	(U21)
cheer up / cheer (sb) up	=	feel happier, or make someone feel happier	(U1)
chicken out	=	become too afraid to do something	(U2)
chill out	=	relax	(U1)
clear up	=	make tidy	(U23)
come across	=	discover by accident	(U3)
come along	=	go somewhere with somebody	(U3)
come down with	=	get an illness	(U23)
come in for	=	receive (criticism or praise)	(U5)
come out	=	become available to buy	(U3)
come round	=	become conscious again	(U23)
come to	=	the total, when added together	(U4)
come up	=	be mentioned in a conversation	(U4)
come up	=	appear on a screen	(U9)
come up with	=	suggest an idea or plan	(U5)
cut down	=	make something fall by using a sharp tool at its base	(U15)
cut down on	=	reduce the number or amount of something	(U12), (U17)
cut off	=	make isolated	(U24)
date back	=	exist since a particular time in the past	(U3)
do away with	=	kill or get rid of	(U13)

do up	=	fix or decorate something, so that it looks good	(U13)
drop out	=	quit a course of study	(U19)
fall for	=	quickly become attracted to somebody	(U2)
fall out	=	have an argument and stop being friends	(U1)
fall through	=	fail to happen	(U19)
feel up to	=	be well or confident enough to do something	(U11)
fight off	=	resist	(U24)
fill in	=	complete a form	(U17)
finish with	=	end a relationship	(U2)
freak out	=	suddenly become very afraid or upset	(U2)
freeze over	=	(the surface of water) turn to ice	(U16)
get (sb) down	=	make someone sad	(U1)
get across	=	succeed in making someone understand something	(U8), (U19)
get at	=	be able to reach something	(U8)
get away	=	to go on holiday or a break	(U7)
get away with	=	not be punished for doing something wrong	(U5), (U13)
get down to	=	start doing something properly	(U17)
get hold of	=	find	(U10)
get in	=	be chosen or accepted into an institution	(U8)
get on	=	have a good relationship with	(U8)
get out of	=	avoid doing something which you don't want to do	(U8)
get over	=	recover from an illness or an upsetting situation	(U2), (U24)
get round to	=	finally do something which you meant to do	(U8)
get through	=	succeed in a competition or exam	(U8)
get through	=	come successfully to the end of a difficult time	(U19)
get together	=	meet with socially	(U11)
get up	=	stand up	(U8)
give away	=	give something to someone for free	(U13)
give up	=	stop doing or trying to do something	(U11)
give yourself up	=	surrender to the police	(U13)
go ahead	=	start to do something	(U4)
go around	=	circulate or spread	(U5)
go by	=	(of time) pass	(U5)
go for	=	try to get	(U20)
go off (sth / sb)	=	stop liking	(U1)
go off	=	make a sudden loud noise	(U14)
go over'	=	look at again, revise	(U20)
go through	=	experience something difficult or unpleasant	(U19)
hack into	=	illegally enter another computer system	(U9)
hand in	=	submit work	(U20)
hand out	=	distribute something among a group	(U20)
hang on	=	wait for a short while	(U7)
hang out	=	spend time with somebody socially	(U7)
hang up	=	stop a telephone conversation	(U7)
head back	=	return	(U21)
hit it off	=	be friendly with someone	(U1)

Phrasal verbs

hold down	=	keep a job	(U17)
hold up	=	rob	(U13)
identify with	=	understand, feel the same as	(U4)
keep to	=	stick with a plan	(U17)
keep up	=	continue	(U17)
keep up with	=	move at the same speed as someone / something	(U12)
key in	=	type information into a computer or other machine	(U10)
knock over	=	hit someone / thing and make them / it fall to the ground (including with a vehicle)	(U11)
let down	=	not do something that someone expects you to do	(U22)
live for	=	have something or someone as the most important thing in your life	(U6)
live on	=	mainly eat a particular kind of food	(U6)
live up to	=	be as good as	(U5)
log in	=	join a computer network	(U10)
log out	=	disconnect from a computer network	(U10)
look back at	=	remember, think about the past	(U3)
look down on	=	think you are better than someone else	(U6)
look into	=	investigate or examine	(U6)
look out for	=	try to notice something or somebody	(U20)
look up	=	find something in a list of things	(U20)
look up to	=	respect and admire	(U6)
make for	=	go towards a place	(U22)
make out	=	be able to see or hear something with difficulty	(U22)
make up for	=	when something good replaces something bad	(U6)
miss out on	=	not have the opportunity to enjoy something	(U6)
move in	=	to start living in a place	(U7)
move on	=	to change the subject you are talking about	(U7)
move on	=	start something new	(U18)
move out	=	to leave the place you live in	(U7)
note down	=	write something so you remember it later	(U20)
own up	=	admit to doing something wrong	(U14)
pass away	=	die	(U13)
pass on	=	tell someone something that another person has told you	(U24)
pass out	=	lose consciousness	(U24)
pick up	=	learn	(U18)
plug in	=	connect a machine to an electricity supply	(U9)
pull in	=	drive your car off the road and into a place	(U21)
pull up	=	(of a vehicle) stop by the road side temporarily	(U23)
put away	=	put somebody in prison	(U14)
put down	=	write someone's name on a document	(U14)
put off	=	make someone dislike something	(U14)
put up with	=	tolerate	(U1), (U16)
read through	=	check something carefully	(U19)
run away	=	leave or escape suddenly	(U14)
run into	=	meet someone by chance	(U11), (U22)
run out	=	use up or finish a supply of something	(U16)
see off	=	say goodbye to someone at an airport, station, etc.	(U22)

see through	=	realise someone is trying to trick you	(U14)
see to	=	deal with something that needs attention	(U14)
set off	=	start a journey	(U22)
set up	=	organise and establish something	(U22)
settle down	=	to start feeling comfortable in a place	(U7)
show around	=	show someone a place	(U11)
show off	=	try to impress other people	(U11)
show up	=	arrive somewhere, usually unexpectedly	(U11)
shut down	=	turn off a computer	(U9)
sleep in	=	get out of bed later than usual	(U12)
slow down	=	go or make something go less quickly	(U15)
soak up	=	take in and hold water	(U16)
speak up	=	talk more loudly	(U9)
spread out over	=	happening over a long period of time	(U4)
stand (sb) up	=	not meet someone you've arranged to meet	(U1)
stand back	=	move a short distance from something	(U12)
stand out	=	be easy to see or notice	(U18)
stand up for	=	defend something or somebody from attack	(U23)
start out	=	begin	(U6)
stay over	=	plan to sleep at someone's house for a night	(U21)
stop over	=	stay at a place on the way to somewhere else	(U21)
switch on	=	turn on a computer, light, etc.	(U9)
take away	=	remove something	(U24)
take off	=	become successful or popular very quickly	(U12)
take off	=	have a short holiday	(U18)
take on	=	employ	(U18)
take out	=	remove money from your bank account	(U18)
take over	=	take control	(U16)
take round	=	walk around a place with somebody to show it to them	(U18)
take up	=	fill an amount of time or space	(U18)
talk (sb) into	=	persuade somebody to do something	(U4)
talk into	=	persuade someone to do something	(U15)
tell off	=	say that someone has done something wrong	(U20)
throw up	=	vomit	(U23)
turn down	=	to make the volume or heat lower	(U10)
turn down	=	reject an invitation	(U12)
turn up	=	to make the volume or heat higher	(U10)
turn up	=	arrive somewhere, sometimes unexpectedly	(U22)
use up	=	take all of something so there is nothing left	(U15)
watch out for	=	pay close attention to something to avoid anything bad happening	(U10)
wear away	=	make smaller or smoother over time	(U16)
wear off	=	slowly stop having an effect	(U24)
wear out	=	make somebody feel very tired	(U16)
wipe out	=	cause to become extinct	(U16)
work on	=	develop and improve	(U17)
work out	=	get an answer or result	(U19)
work out	=	exercise	(U21)

(be / make) aware **of**	(U15)	**by** far	(U3), (U22)	**on** sb's behalf	(U6)
(be) accused **of**	(U14)	**by** heart	(U3)	**on** the phone	(U9)
(be) **against** sth	(U20)	concentrate **on**	(U2)	pop **over**	(U17)
(be) **against** the law	(U13), (U20)	confess **to**	(U13)	protection **from**	(U15)
(be) ashamed **of**	(U1)	cope **with**	(U15)	rely **on**	(U16)
(be) **at** a loose end	(U11)	day **by** day	(U4)	respond **to**	(U2)
(be) **at** sea	(U22)	deep **down**	(U1)	result **in**	(U9), (U16)
(be) **at** the airport	(U1)	discourage **from**	(U15)	ride **up** and **down**	(U23)
(be) bad **for** sth	(U9)	do **without**	(U10)	sentence sb **to** sth	(U13)
(be) banned **from** sth	(U14)	drive **at** (speed)	(U22)	speak **over** the intercom	(U19)
(be) exposed **to**	(U16)	equipped **with**	(U10)	stand **in** line	(U21)
(be) **in** agony	(U23)	experiment **with** sth	(U10)	suffer **from**	(U9)
(be) responsible **for**	(U2)	feel anger **towards** sb	(U18)	suspect sb **of** sth	(U24)
(be) satisfied **with**	(U15)	feel **under** the weather	(U23)	threat **of**	(U14)
(be) **under** arrest	(U13)	find sb guilty **of** sth	(U13)	**throughout** an event	(U15)
(be) **under** attack	(U17)	focus **on**	(U2)	**to** sb's astonishment	(U18)
(be) **under** control	(U17)	follow **in** sb's footsteps	(U5)	travel **by** car	(U6)
(be) **under** pressure	(U23)	**for** a change	(U8)	**under** control	(U22)
(be) **under** suspicion	(U13)	**for** real	(U12)	**under** pressure	(U6)
(be) **up** and **about**	(U23)	**for** the moment	(U8), (U12)	**under** the impression	(U6)
(be) **within**	(U21)	**from** time **to** time	(U19)	**upon** arrival	(U1)
(be) wrong **with** sb	(U12), (U22)	get **on** sb's nerves	(U1)	win **at** all costs	(U18)
a combination **of**	(U12)	get sick **of**	(U24)	with reference **to**	(U3)
a smile **upon** sb's face	(U18)	glance **through**	(U17)	**within** budget	(U12)
a steep rise **in**	(U16)	go **to** hospital **with**	(U22)	**within** the next few days	(U10)
advantage **of** sth	(U7)	hide **from** sight	(U14)	**without** a doubt	(U10)
after all	(U20)	immune **to**	(U24)	**without** delay	(U6)
after sth	(U20)	**in** connection **with**	(U3)	years **from** now	(U10)
all **over**	(U17), (U19)	**in** favour **of**	(U4)		(U19)
allergic **to**	(U24)	**in** general	(U3)		
along the road	(U20)	**in** other words	(U4)		
among other things	(U7)	**in** private	(U5)		
among the most …	(U7)	**in** public	(U5)		
appeal **to** sb	(U11)	**in** search **of**	(U21)		
arrange **for**	(U9)	**in** secret	(U8)		
arrest sb **for** sth	(U14)	**in** writing	(U8)		
as a matter **of** fact	(U8)	increase **by**	(U4)		
as a result **of**	(U7)	just **for** sth	(U12)		
as far **as**	(U8)	know all **along**	(U20)		
at a price	(U5)	lack **of**	(U24)		
at fault	(U4)	lead **to**	(U2)		
at risk **of**	(U4), (U9)	let sb **through**	(U17)		
at sb's disposal	(U3)	move **on**	(U11)		
attitude **towards** sb	(U18)	object **to**	(U16)		
behind the scenes	(U5)	**off** the coast	(U19)		
benefit **from**	(U24)	**on** a daily basis	(U7)		
break a leg **in** two places	(U1)	**on** account **of**	(U6)		
burst **into** tears	(U2)	**on** condition that	(U7)		
by all accounts	(U5)	**on** second thoughts	(U11)		

Collocations and expressions

(be / get) stuck in traffic	(U22)	get straight to the point	(U20)
(be) a bad influence on	(U1)	get the feeling	(U20)
(be) brain dead	(U19)	get under sb's skin	(U2)
(be) held	(U4)	ghost town	(U7)
(be) in agony	(U2)	give a speech	(U4)
(be) lost for words	(U2)	give birth	(U24)
(be) none of one's business	(U10)	give sb an idea	(U22)
(be) on good terms with each other	(U2)	give sb the sack	(U17)
(be) on the edge of one's seat	(U2)	give sth a go	(U13)
(be) on the increase	(U8)	go bungee jumping	(U11)
(be) out of breath	(U24)	go climbing	(U11)
(be) widely known	(U4)	go on strike	(U17)
all over the place	(U7)	go to town on sth	(U7)
answering machine	(U9)	have no choice	(U13)
apply cream	(U23)	have roots in sth	(U3)
as busy as a bee	(U16)	have sth in common	(U22)
at one's convenience	(U10)	have sth on one's brain	(U19)
best of both worlds	(U7)	hold a place in one's heart	(U12)
beyond one's control	(U10)	hold one's breath	(U23)
boarding pass	(U21)	household name	(U6)
brainstorm	(U19)	in-flight entertainment	(U21)
brainwave	(U19)	jump at the chance	(U18)
break sb's heart	(U1)	keep an eye on sth	(U14)
break the law	(U13)	keep in shape	(U24)
build a good relationship	(U4)	keep one's promise	(U20)
build a reputation	(U3)	keep sb company	(U20)
build an empire	(U3)	know better than to do sth	(U1)
cabin crew	(U21)	knowing one's luck	(U18)
cash machine	(U9)	lead the way	(U5)
catch a cold	(U23)	let the cat out of the bag	(U16)
catch sb's attention	(U10)	life sentence	(U14)
change one's ways	(U14)	live life in the fast lane	(U8)
claim to fame	(U6)	lose one's passion	(U5)
come close to	(U12)	lose one's voice	(U23)
come out of nowhere	(U6)	lose track of time	(U14)
community service	(U14)	make a difference	(U12)
convey apologies to sb	(U1)	make a fool of oneself	(U1), (U13)
couldn't care less	(U13)	make no difference	(U10)
cry crocodile tears	(U16)	make sb redundant	(U17)
departure gate	(U21)	miss the deadline	(U17)
do damage to	(U3)	never get anywhere	(U6)
do justice	(U14)	not know the first thing about sth	(U12)
do karate	(U11)	open doors for sb	(U6)
do one's bit	(U15)	overhead compartment	(U21)
do sb good	(U24)	paint everyone with the same brush	(U18)
do yoga	(U11)	pick sb's brains	(U18)
draw attention to oneself	(U5)	play a part	(U15)
drop litter	(U15)	play a role	(U3)
excess baggage	(U21)	play by ear	(U4)
face doing sth	(U1)	play chess	(U11)
fish for compliments	(U16)	play volleyball	(U11)
get a promotion	(U17)		

put an end to sth	(U15)
put limits on sth	(U22)
put one's life at risk	(U12)
put oneself in sb's shoes	(U18)
rack one's brains	(U19)
resist the temptation	(U8)
save space	(U4)
see the funny side	(U5)
seize the chance	(U5)
set an example	(U5)
sewing machine	(U9)
skip breakfast	(U23)
tackle a problem	(U15)
take a trip	(U22)
take action	(U15)
take into consideration	(U7), (U10)
take oneself too seriously	(U12)
take pleasure in something	(U20)
take responsibility	(U13)
take sb's temperature	(U23)
take sb's word for something	(U20)
take the initiative	(U17)
talk of the town	(U7)
the brains behind sth	(U19)
the secret of sb's success	(U6)
think on one's feet	(U18)
time machine	(U9)
upset stomach	(U24)
urban jungle	(U8)
use without permission	(U3)
vending machine	(U9)
walk of life	(U8)
washing machine	(U9)
what the future holds	(U22)
with regret	(U2)
without fail	(U8)
wolf in sheep's clothing	(U16)
worm the information out of sb	(U16)
You are what you eat!	(U24)

Word formation

Adjective → adjective		
TINY	TINIEST	U10

Adjective → noun		
ABSENT	ABSENCE	U20
ANXIOUS	ANXIETY	U2
BRAVE	BRAVERY	U9
DIFFERENT	DIFFERENCE	U2
DISTANT	DISTANCE	U2
EQUAL	EQUALITY	U21
FESTIVE	FESTIVITIES	U3
FIT	FITNESS	U2
FRIENDLY	UNFRIENDLINESS	U20
HONEST	DISHONESTY	U12
KIND	KINDNESS	U10
LAZY	LAZINESS	U18
MAD	MADNESS	U2
ORIGINAL	ORIGINS	U3
POPULAR	POPULARITY	U2
REAL	REALITY	U10, U24
RESPONSIBLE	RESPONSIBILITY	U18
SAFE	SAFETY	U2
SICK	SICKNESS	U24
STRONG	STRENGTH	U2
TENSE	TENSION	U2
TRADITIONAL	TRADITIONS	U3
TRUE	TRUTH	U2
WEAK	WEAKNESS	U11

Adjective → opposite adjective		
ATTRACTIVE	UNATTRACTIVE	U7
FORMAL	INFORMAL	U7
HONEST	DISHONEST	U7
LEGAL	ILLEGAL	U7, U13
LIKELY	UNLIKELY	U7
MORAL	IMMORAL	U22
ORDINARY	EXTRAORDINARY	U7
ORGANISED	DISORGANISED	U7
POLITE	IMPOLITE	U7
POSSIBLE	IMPOSSIBLE	U12
REGULAR	IRREGULAR	U7
RESPONSIBLE	IRRESPONSIBLE	U7

Adjective → verb		
SPECIAL	SPECIALISE	U11

Adverbs		
ACCIDENT	ACCIDENTALLY	U10
ALPHABET	ALPHABETICALLY	U22
ATTRACTIVE	UNATTRACTIVELY	U16
AUTOMATIC	AUTOMATICALLY	U8
CARE	CARELESSLY	U8
COMFORT	COMFORTABLY	U8
CONSCIOUS	UNCONSCIOUSLY	U8
CONSIDER	CONSIDERABLY	U21
CONTINUE	CONTINUOUSLY	U24
CONTROVERSY	CONTROVERSIALLY	U16
DANGER	DANGEROUSLY	U8
EXTRAORDINARY	EXTRAORDINARILY	U8
FOOL	FOOLISHLY	U16
FURY	FURIOUSLY	U16
GENERAL	GENERALLY	U8
GUILT	GUILTILY	U16
IRRITATE	IRRITATINGLY	U16
MEMORY	MEMORABLY	U16
OFFEND	OFFENSIVELY	U8
REPEAT	REPEATEDLY	U8
SKILL	SKILFULLY	U16
STEADY	STEADILY	U8
SUIT	SUITABLY	U19
THOUGHT	THOUGHTFULLY	U12
TRUE	TRULY	U10
USUAL	UNUSUALLY	U22
VIRTUAL	VIRTUALLY	U10
VISIBLE	INVISIBLY	U24

Noun → adjective

AMAZEMENT	AMAZED	U1
COLOUR	COLOURFUL	U24
CONFIDENCE	CONFIDENT	U1
DANGER	ENDANGERED	U15
DESPAIR	DESPERATE	U1
DRAMA	DRAMATIC	U15, U23
ECOLOGY	ECOLOGICAL	U15, U23
EMBARRASSMENT	EMBARRASSED	U1
END	ENDLESS	U12
FRUSTRATION	FRUSTRATED	U1
GUILT	GUILTY	U1
ICE	ICY	U22
JOY	OVERJOYED	U1
LUCK	LUCKY	U9
MASS	MASSIVE	U15
MEMORY	MEMORABLE	U11
MUD	MUDDY	U21
OPTION	OPTIONAL	U23
PAIN	PAINFUL	U23
POWER	POWERFUL	U9
PRICE	PRICELESS	U21
PROFIT	PROFITABLE	U23
REASON	REASONABLE	U20
RELIEF	RELIEVED	U1
RESIDENT	RESIDENTIAL	U23
RIDICULE	RIDICULOUS	U23
RUST	RUSTY	U23
SENSE	SENSITIVE	U1
SYMPATHY	SYMPATHETIC	U1
TRICK	TRICKIEST	U19
WIRE	WIRELESS	U9

Noun → noun

ACT	ACTION	U6
BAKER	BAKERY	U6
BLOG	BLOGGERS	U6
BURGLAR	BURGLARY	U13
CHAMPION	CHAMPIONSHOP	U20
CHARACTER	CHARACTERISTIC	U6
CRIME	CRIMINAL	U13
CRITIC	CRITICISM	U6
ECONOMY	ECONOMIST	U12
EXAM	EXAMINER	U6
FRIEND	FRIENDSHIP	U6
JOURNAL	JOURNALISM	U22
MEMBER	MEMBERSHIP	U11
MOTOR	MOTORISTS	U21
NATION	NATIONALITY	U6
NOVEL	NOVELIST	U19
PARTNER	PARTNERSHIP	U9
PRESENT	PRESENCE	U12
SCIENCE	SCIENTISTS	U6
SPONSOR	SPONSORSHIP	U6
TERROR	TERRORISM	U13

Noun → verb

APOLOGY	APOLOGISE	U4
CLASS	CLASSIFY	U4
COURAGE	ENCOURAGE	U4
CRITIC	CRITICISE	U4
MEMORY	MEMORISE	U20
PROOF	PROVE	U4
RELIEF	RELIEVE	U4
SUCCESS	SUCCEED	U4
TERROR	TERRORISE	U4

Prefixes

ADVANTAGE	DISADVANTAGE	U18
AGREE	DISAGREE	U12
APPEAR	DISAPPEAR	U17
APPROVE	DISAPPROVAL	U17
BUILD	REBUILD	U17
CREDIBLE	INCREDIBLE	U17
EMPLOY	UNEMPLOYED	U17
LIKE	DISLIKE	U11
PATIENT	IMPATIENT	U17
PAY	REPAY	U17
UNDERSTAND	MISUNDERSTANDING	U17
WRITE	REWRITE	U22

Word formation

Verb → noun		
AMAZE	AMAZEMENT	U11
ANALYSE	ANALYST	U18
ASSESS	ASSESSMENT	U19
ATTACH	ATTACHMENT	U9
COINCIDE	COINCIDENCE	U22
CONCLUDE	CONCLUSION	U14
CONNECT	CONNECTION	U21
CONSULT	CONSULTANT	U21
CORRECT	CORRECTIONS	U20
DECIDE	DECISION	U14
DELIVER	DELIVERY	U18
DETERMINE	DETERMINATION	U5
DISABLE	DISABILITY	U24
DISCOVER	DISCOVERY	U19
ENCOURAGE	ENCOURAGEMENT	U5, U20
FAIL	FAILURE	U5
GOVERN	GOVERNMENT	U9
GRADUATE	GRADUATION	U19
INFLUENCE	INFLUENCE	U5
INSPIRE	INSPIRATION	U5
JUDGE	JUDGEMENT	U18
LAND	LANDING	U21
OCCUPY	OCCUPATION	U14
OFFEND	OFFENCE	U13
OFFEND	OFFENDER	U14
OPERATE	OPERATION	U14
PERFORM	PERFORMERS	U10
PHOTOGRAPH	PHOTOGRAPHER	U14
PREFER	PREFERENCE	U12
PROVE	PROOF	U14
PUNISH	PUNISHMENT	U13
REACT	REACTION	U24
REALISE	REALITY	U5
RECEIVE	RECEPTION	U3
REFER	REFERENCE	U20
REFLECT	REFLECTION	U22
RELATE	RELATIONSHIP	U18
RETIRE	RETIREMENT	U18
ROB	ROBBERY	U13
SIGNIFY	SIGNIFICANCE	U14
SPECTATE	SPECTACLE	U3
SPONSOR	SPONSOR	U5
SUCCEED	SUCCESS	U5
SURVIVE	SURVIVORS	U24

Verb → adjective		
ACCEPT	UNACCEPTABLE	U15
AMAZE	AMAZING	U9
BENEFIT	BENEFICIAL	U19
COMPETE	COMPETITIVE	U11
EDUCATE	EDUCATIONAL	U15
HELP	UNHELPFUL	U19
LIVE	ALIVE	U10
RENEW	RENEWABLE	U15
SIGNIFY	SIGNIFICANT	U3
SUIT	SUITABLE	U3
SUSPECT	SUSPICIOUS	U11, U13
USE	USELESS	U15
VARY	VARIOUS	U3

NATIONAL GEOGRAPHIC LEARNING

National Geographic Learning,
a Cengage Company

**New Close-up English in Use B2 Student's Book,
Second Edition**
Author: David McKeegan

Additional material: Helen Kidd

Program Director: Sharon Jervis

Editorial Manager: Claire Merchant

Project Manager: Adele Moss

Head of Strategic Marketing: Charlotte Ellis

Head of Production and Design: Celia Jones

Content Project Manager: Nick Lowe

Manufacturing Manager: Eyvett Davis

Cover Design: Geoff Ward

Compositors: Jonathan Bargus, Elisabeth Heissler,
and Geoff Ward

For permission to use material from this text or product,
submit all requests online at **cengage.com/permissions**
Further permissions questions can be emailed to
permissionrequest@cengage.com

Student's Edition:
ISBN: 978-1-473-78636-3

National Geographic Learning
Cheriton House, North Way,
Andover, Hampshire, SP10 5BE
United Kingdom

Locate your local office at **international.cengage.com/region**

Visit National Geographic Learning online at **ELTNGL.com**
Visit our corporate website at **www.cengage.com**

CREDITS

Photos: 10 © Westend61/Getty Images; **16** © SpeedKingz/Shutterstock; **43** © monkeybusinessimages/iStockphoto; **49** © fizkes/iStockphoto; **50** © your personal camera obscura/Moment/Getty Images; **51** © CoffeeAndMilk/E+/Getty Images; **61** © anyaivanova/Shutterstock; **67** © peshkov/iStockphoto; **68** © narvikk/iStockphoto; **73** © IM_photo/Shutterstock; **79** © shannonstent/iStockphoto; **80** © imagenavi/Getty Images; **101** © anatoliy_gleb/Shutterstock; **106** balipadma/Shutterstock; **110** © amenic181/iStockphoto; **126** © Africa Studio/Shutterstock; **129** © Panther Media GmbH/Alamy Stock Photo; **149** © Ashraf Salah Eldin/Eyeem/Getty Images; **150** © Ghulam Hussain/iStockphoto; **155** © simonkr//iStockphoto; **157** © Johan Swanepoel/Alamy Stock Photo; **161** © Tashi-Delek/iStockphoto; **162** © FatCamera/iStockphoto.

ON THE COVER

The cover image shows the ceiling of the lobby in the Burj Al Arab hotel in Dubai. It is one of the world's tallest and most luxurious hotels. Guests can choose from seventeen different pillows for the perfect night's sleep!
© Nick Fewings/Unsplash

Printed in Greece by Bakis, SA
Print Number: 01   Print Year: 2022